QUARTER TURNS

SMALL SHIFTS, BIG IMPACT

BY: TIM FURLONG

www.MyQuarterTurns.com

Publishing services provided by  **Archangel Ink**

ISBN: 1517511070
ISBN-13: 978-1517511074

In memory of Rosemarie Rothe (1942–2013)
My teacher and the ultimate lifelong learner…

This book is dedicated to my family.

Without you, I would lack the courage to start, the persistence to continue, and the joy that comes from sharing my life with my best friends.

Contents

"*Forward*" By Rob Otte

I'm honored Tim asked me to write a foreword for his book. I'm also honored you're reading my "*forward*."

I choose the word "*forward*" for my introduction because that word has energy, and that energy points in a good direction. Tim is an energy guy, and he helps people get pointed in a good direction.

I also like the word *forward* here because it's a small shift from *foreword,* and that small shift makes an impact.

Tim helps people find ways to make small shifts—or "Quarter Turns"—for big impact. Through his coaching and writing, Tim helps me understand energy, make small shifts, and move forward. Reading this collection of Tim's writings can help you do the same.

To get started in a positive way, I suggest you take some action. It's an action Tim has asked me to take countless times, and it always helps me have a better experience with what follows. It's an action because it's full of choice, and choice is full of action. It's four words.

Tell me something good.

Read on to learn more.

Preface

I was the youngest in my immediate family of seven children. As I got older, I came to understand that being the youngest in a large Italian family with a doting mother and four sisters would explain the ease of my childhood.

My youth was filled with love and laughter even after the divorce of my parents at an early age. While I realize the separation of parents can create all kinds of challenges, I was fortunate because it allowed me to grow up with two very involved fathers.

Alan, my stepfather, was a model of patience, routine, and consistency. He taught me the value of working hard at something, being persistent, and seeing a task all the way through to completion. I think his engineering background helped me understand that I do not need to accomplish the grand plan all in one day. As long as I can finish one small piece and pay attention to most of the details, I have done a good day's work and am one step closer to my goal.

"Fuzz," my father, lived across the state line almost two hours away. Though I was only able to see him one weekend a month and over the holidays, he was always close by in my thoughts. Fuzz was there to celebrate all of my accomplishments, rarely missing an important game or event. He was there to witness my first home run, my first days of school, my graduation—all the things one would expect a father to do. My favorite times were usually found driving to a ball game, sitting around the dinner table after a good meal, or just ""talking ball" at a local restaurant.

I was what we might now call a hyperactive kid, and I had a hard time sitting still. My quick wit and smile allowed me to get away with most anything, and I rarely found my way into any serious trouble. Both of my dads recognized this about me early on, and they were quick to point out that charm and personality would only get me so far in this life. I had better start working on something else to apply that charisma to besides goofing off.

Both Alan and Fuzz knew how to push me to do a little better, although not in ways you may think of as traditional. Alan was a man who preferred to use only a few words and would often ask me questions about the choices I had made or the decisions I was about to make. Those questions caused me to own up to some of my mistakes or helped me clarify the direction I was heading.

Fuzz, on the other hand, was a man of many words and liked to tell stories to get his point across. He would often quote his grandfather, "Dodo," who used to tell him in a broken Italian tongue, "Get up and take a walk around the block," which meant get off your butt and go do something productive, or my favorite, "You go to school for kill the time," which I think speaks for itself.

The best piece of advice Fuzz gave me was probably unintentional. Fuzz was always looking for ways to communicate in codes. He liked efficiency and could usually figure out the quickest way to get something done with the least amount of resistance; something he passed along to me. Often, when my siblings or I were not performing at our best, he would say, "Tighten up your chin strap a few notches," an old football reference meaning, "Get your head on straight and sharpen up." Over the years, that saying morphed into a piercing look, a slight nod, tight lips, and two words . . . "*Quarter Turn*."

These two words have helped me make sense of all the lessons I have learned in life, and these two words have made all the difference to me. I have spent the last twenty-five years of my life searching for those "Quarter Turns" and helping others uncover their own. And in helping others, I have discovered many more of my own Quarter Turns along the way.

Introduction

What is a Quarter Turn?

"Quarter Turns" are the little things that can have a massive impact on your life. Often seemingly small and insignificant, they can totally alter your perspective and completely change you as a result. The application of these Quarter Turns creates real, meaningful, and sustainable change in your life, your business, and your relationships.

These two words have made a significant difference in my own life journey. By tuning in and learning from my own Quarter Turns, I have grown in ways I would have never thought possible. As I reflected on my growth, I was inspired to bring the Quarter Turns concept to the world, hoping to empower others to pay heed to their own Quarter Turns and make their own quantum life leaps.

I am fortunate to have had many brilliant teachers in my life. Interestingly, the Quarter Turns impacting me most have usually come from the rich blend of people with whom I have surrounded myself. I believe the same people and experiences exist in everyone's life, and it is my hope that this book will encourage you to tune into the Quarter Turns in your life that will make all the difference for you.

Big, sweeping changes are often difficult to quantify and only come about every so often. When they do, they usually have less impact than we anticipated. I believe the little things—the slight adjustments and minor corrections we all make every day—are where the magic in our lives exists. We simply need to pay attention in order to reap the rewards.

How to Use This Book

Understanding and applying your own Quarter Turns will allow you to design a more fulfilling and successful life. As a coach and facilitator, I felt the need to organize my philosophy into something more methodical, so I can help others focus on specific aspects to solve problems and improve. My program has five basic sections:

1) Awareness
2) Clarity
3) Obstacles
4) Strategy
5) Sustainability

With these five steps, I've structured the book much the same way that I would structure a coaching relationship. Yet like a true coaching program, there is no one way that works the best for everyone, as we are all unique. This book is designed for you to open any section and read the Quarter Turn and with it a call to action that will help you apply the lesson and create the most value for you in the process.

So welcome to my *Quarter Turns*! I hope these lessons will be as much service to you on your journey as they have been for me!

My Story

I'm Gonna Play in the Majors

When I was ten years old, like many of my friends, I wanted to be a professional baseball player. I played baseball almost every day I could. Sometimes, when there was no one to throw the ball with, I would go out in our backyard and toss the ball around to myself, flying across the lawn to make diving, game-saving catches over and over again.

In fourth grade, I was finally allowed to play hardball, and life was good. I was one of the best players on the team. I could pitch, catch, play shortstop, first base, outfield—you name it, I played it. I still remember my first home run at old Burns Park. It was a hard line drive past the second baseman and the right fielder, and with no fence behind him, I crossed home before the outfielder ever got the ball.

As I got older, I had my first tryout in junior high school to make the team. What a nerve-racking experience that was. All these kids trying out, and cut lists posted at the end of the week. I remember hoping and praying to see my name on the list each week. Finally, the last list went up; I had made the team. I can still remember today what a great feeling that was.

The next year we won the city championship in "a come from behind" game. With two outs in the last inning and one man on, I battled for thirteen pitches until I drilled a triple into left field. I ended up scoring on a single, and we won later that inning.

Everything was going according to the plan. I was on my way to high school, then college, then off to the big time. Life seemed perfect. That is, until I got to high school and realized that most everyone who played baseball was a lot bigger and better than I.

During tryouts, I noticed how the ball seemed to jump off some of the kids' bats and how they could throw the ball like it was shot out of a cannon, seemingly without any real effort at all. That drove me to work twice as hard, to hustle, and do all the little things that make a great player great. The problem was that no matter how hard I worked and how much extra effort I put in, some kids were just physically gifted, and I could not keep up with them.

Despite that, I worked my butt off and made the team. I also developed a better understanding of the expression "riding the pine." For the first time in my life, when the season started, I was relegated to the bench. I got in a few games pinch running, and I even started a few. I did well, made all the plays, and hit a walk-off game winning single that year. Even with that, by the end of the season I could see the writing on the wall.

My junior year, I worked all through the winter, determined to make the varsity squad and be a contributor. I had a great tryout. I outhustled and outworked most everyone there. I made cut after cut, and I knew all the hard work was going pay off. Then, on the last day of tryouts, I was called into the coach's office. It was there I received the news that would change everything. I found out I was the last man cut prior to beginning the season.

"Wow, that's it," I thought. Over, kaput. There was such finality about it.

I remember sitting alone in the locker room and starting to cry. Looking back, I wasn't crying about not making the team. I was crying because it was the end of the dream I had envisioned and lived out in my head for so many years. With one piece of news from the coach, all that was gone.

My first big Quarter Turn came from that experience. I realized that no matter how hard I worked at something, or how much effort I put in, if I put that energy into something that is not part of my life's purpose, I am destined to come up short.

I realized I could have hit baseballs every day, all day, for years. I could have worked with every coach in the country. I could have studied films, trained right, eaten right, and done everything else right, and it still wouldn't change the fact that I wasn't going to play in the major leagues.

The good news is that getting cut from the team got me focused full-time on another activity that I was slowly beginning to get into—music.

I Wanna Be a Rock Star

While still in high school, I formed a band and sang at gigs on a sporadic basis at the high school and around the University of Michigan campus. Until I got cut from the baseball team, I had only thought playing in a band would be a great way to meet girls. Now, with all my newfound free time, I started to really focus on the band.

Interestingly, I soon realized I was good at it. Within six months, I played my first two thousand-seat venue. And it just kept going from there. We rapidly became local favorites and developed a small following. With very little effort, I was seeing success.

I wondered what would happen if I applied myself to music the same way I did to baseball. So I did, and sure enough—things started moving forward fast. Soon I was asked to play in a larger, more established band. From there my band put out an independent record and began to tour.

My dream shifted from being a pro baseball player to getting a major recording contract, releasing a hit record, getting on MTV, selling a million records, and touring the country. Those were some amazing years for me, and my band had some early success. We played gigs all around the country, had our songs played on different radio stations, opened for major recording artists, played a twenty thousand-seat arena, won contests, and even got to play in Moscow!

The dream was beginning to take shape. Major labels began contacting us and showing up at various gigs. I thought it was only a matter of time before I'd say, "Hey, I'm a rock star!"

Then something happened that again put an abrupt halt to the plan—grunge music.

Damn that Kurt Cobain!

Please understand, Nirvana and the Seattle sound was a great thing for music. It just wasn't great for me.

Just to clarify, we were not some sort of hair band, wearing spandex and putting make-up on our faces. We also were not a grunge band, and that was our undoing. Although we kept at it for a few more years, eventually the band disintegrated, and all of us moved on. I found myself back in college to finish up a degree.

Though it was a tough lesson to swallow at the time, I had learned my next big Quarter Turn: no matter how great your product is, timing is everything. I'm sure there were a lot of cell phone manufacturers that had some really great visions for phones in 2007, and then a little device called the iPhone came out. When it did, the playing field or stage changed forever. Many would-be big leaguers got benched, and many potential megastars found the fans screaming for the next big thing.

Looking back now, it was probably a blessing. Not getting signed to a major label again allowed me to move on to other interests much sooner; interests that were better aligned with what I would discover was my calling. I have to tell you, though, it sure didn't feel like a blessing at the time.

I Wanna Find My Purpose

So there I was, not a major league baseball player and not a singer in a rock and roll band. As far as I was concerned, I didn't have much to show for a lot of dedication and hard work, and I was somewhat discouraged.

I went back to college, finished up my degree, and almost instantly landed a job with an old friend, working in sales. As it turns out, being a musician was a great foundation for sales because I had already learned to handle rejection very well!

I also learned I was a natural at sales and had a great background for it. I drew on my experience as a musician and took my performance from a stage with an audience to a desk or a kitchen table with one or two people. In both contexts I was performing, only now I was actually getting paid for it.

It didn't take long for the owners of the company I worked for to notice. Within a few years, I was asked if I would be interested in training new salespeople that entered the organization. Thinking this would be a great way to get back in front of a crowd, I agreed, as long as I could do the training in front of a group rather than one-on-one. The owners said yes and just like that I was on stage again, beginning an entirely new career.

The training was a hit, and not just with new salespeople but with the established veterans as well. Since salespeople tend to change companies, soon word got around, and I was asked to provide training all over the region. This eventually led to me being asked if I would consider coaching salespeople one-on-one.

It was then that my path and my purpose started to become clearer to me.

Right about that time, when my sales training and coaching business began to take shape, I got a call from my sister Ann. She asked me to help her with a small human resource and training-consulting firm she had recently launched. It was a natural fit, and the door to working with companies outside my comfort zone of sales organizations was now wide open.

I probably didn't realize it back then, but all the work I had done up to that point had prepared me for my life's purpose. The challenges and struggles I faced were put there to guide me toward that purpose, even though it wasn't yet defined.

In my coaching practice, I often challenge my clients to take a look back at their own story, just as I have. I ask them to identify those defining moments and Quarter Turns that helped shape who they are today and, more importantly, how those moments helped put them on the path toward their life's purpose.

After all, it's difficult to decide where you want to go until you can appreciate and accept where you've been.

Section 1

Awareness

From my perspective as a coach, creating awareness and being self-aware are some of the more valuable actions that you can engage yourself in when it comes to making real and significant changes in your life.

- How are you showing up, in your business, in your life, and in your relationships?
- What is the impact you are creating for yourself and those around you?
- What are your tendencies, and what decisions do you make on a consistent basis?

Recognition of patterns and habits that define your life is a useful piece of knowledge if you ever plan to break some habits that aren't working for you. Being highly self-aware of who you are and how you behave in critical moments goes a long way toward developing habits that are more in line with your goals and becoming the person that you plan to be.

What irritates you? What excites you? What triggers an emotional response in you, good or bad? What stresses you out? What causes you to say or do things that you later regret? What are the habits that you value the most about yourself, and which have gotten you all the best results in your life? Are you sticking with them?

Being aware can help begin the process of unlocking the answers to these important questions, and it all starts by simply tuning into you.

Do you ever feel like you are going against the grain or constantly swimming upstream like a salmon?

Becoming aware can help you understand why and help you identify a strategy to start going with the flow instead of against it.

Start today by paying attention to how you feel when you wake up. Take temperature checks throughout the day; get a sense of when you are at your peak and when your energy levels are drained.

Ask yourself "why."

Making the first Quarter Turn of awareness is more about the process of asking the right questions rather than always having the right answers.

Tell Me Something Good

I begin every coaching conversation, every seminar, and every conference with this request: "Tell me something good." So I thought this would be a great way to start this first major section on awareness. "Something good" can be anything that has happened to you recently, something you like, something or anything in your life that is good, be it work, play, family, or — whatever. Maybe it's something that has just happened, or it could be something that is about to. I can tell you that sometimes it takes people a while to come up with that "good thing," but they always do, and so can you.

Something you will learn about me is that I don't do things randomly or just for the sake of doing them. There is always a meaning and a purpose. Why would I start every engagement with that same statement? It's an interesting request, but from my experience working with high performers, human nature wires us to focus on the one or two things that are going wrong instead of the many hundreds of things that are going right. Since our brains are wired for sameness, this type of thinking can actually become a habit. The idea is to get you into the habit of being intentional and starting off each day, week, or month by reminding yourself of something good.

As you engage in this process, notice what happens to your state of mind. As you think about your son or daughter accomplishing something really great, or the visit you just had with a friend or relative, or that really special item you just acquired, didn't you just change the way you feel? Most will say yes. Just thinking about something good changes our state and usually for the better. The more important question to ask yourself is: "Who" actually changed your state? You did.

It's extremely powerful to realize that we have 100 percent control over our emotional state, and we can change our energy and attitude simply by thinking about and recognizing all the good things that are really happening in our lives. In fact, I believe it's one of the few things we have total control over.

From my perspective, there are two types of people in the world. One type is those individuals who believe they have no say in how their day is going to go—they just wake up and it's like a pinball machine bumping them around from task to task, crisis to crisis.

The other type is those people who seem to show up every day, by design and on purpose, with the right energy and the right attitude. Which type do you want to be?

I am a big believer in energy and include the topic in many of my talks. Ask yourself this: Do you know somebody who, every single day, either in business or in life, shows up with the wrong energy? Do you enjoy being around that person? Didn't think so.

You probably also know somebody who seems to create a different type of experience. You see them and instantly perk up—you know you are going to have a great day. Maybe it's someone who walks into your workspace or a social gathering and when they enter the room . . . WOW, you just know you are going to have a better experience simply because this person is present. Think about that for a minute. Certain people can actually change the energy in the room. What type of person are you?

The kind of energy you bring with you and how you show up every day is really dependent upon one person and one person only—you. So go on, tell me something good.

Ask yourself:

- What type of energy am I showing up with every day? Is it the right energy?
- How am I showing up in my business and in my life? Is it how I want to show up?
- What impact am I having on those around me?
- Each day this week, take a few minutes to think about or write out your something good; notice what happens. Notice if you feel better.

Knowing and believing that your energy is actually a choice that you get to make every single day is the first and most important Quarter Turn you can make.

What is Your Brand?

Many of us are affiliated with companies and organizations that have identified their core values. In fact, you can probably find copies of them posted on the walls, framed in pictures, on posters, pocket cards, T-shirts, you name it. The problem is, if you were to ask most people what those core values actually are, they couldn't even begin to tell you, and they certainly couldn't tell you what they stood for. In fact, I would guess that most organizations have the core value of respect posted boldly somewhere, but if you look around the organization, how much respect is actually being demonstrated?

With that in mind, I would like you to identify your own personal core values. In these values, what I really mean is, if I went to purchase you at the store, what is your "brand"? If you were out shopping, would you be interested in your brand, or would you pass on it in favor of another brand?

A core value is not a "need to" or a "should have," but an absolute, non-negotiable, must-have ingredient in your personal brand. You'll know it's a core value because when you write it and it's currently not something you are living, you will have a powerful reaction—a major "aha" that you need to get this in your life ASAP. Or if it's already a part of your life, you would have an extremely difficult time compromising it for any reason.

Once you have identified your personal core values, decide what they actually mean to you. Define them and explain them in great detail.

I''ll share an example.

My first core value has and always will be devotion to my family, but my definition of family may not be the same as yours.

First and foremost, my wife and two boys are always the most important to me. Every decision I make in my life has an impact on them and if that impact isn't positive, it not only affects them, it also impacts me as well. I know this because my energy level depletes and I feel drained and exhausted, like something just isn't quite right. This is how I know it's a true core value and part of my brand, because when I do not honor it in the appropriate manner it impacts me at so many levels. I have a large immediate family as well with brothers, sisters, stepbrothers, stepsisters, aunts, uncles, parents, stepparents, etc. I also have a huge network of close friends and business partners, as well as individuals I have coached or been coached by over the years who fit into my large extended family. These people have all touched my life in many ways and are extremely important to me. For them I am unwilling to compromise, even just a little, because I know how I would feel if I did.

Do you see how I can define and explain that core value, and can you tell how important it is to me? Get clear on who you are and what you are about. Like a product at the store, what is your brand?

Over the years, I have found that getting clear on your core values can be life impacting and, in some cases, life altering. Once you are crystal clear on who you are and what you stand for, difficult decisions and forks in the road become much easier to make and navigate. Usually one road is not consistent with your core values.

I have also found the opposite to be true; those of us unclear on our core values tend to find a general sense of uneasiness when one of those core values is violated or not being honored in some way. It's not that something is wrong, but something just isn't quite right, which creates an underlying tension. Being able to identify what is challenging you at your job, in a relationship, or anywhere else in your life empowers you to make rational, intelligent choices based on who you are. Making this Quarter Turn can confirm in your gut that you have chosen the right path.

Ask yourself:

- What's my brand?
- What do I stand for?
- What am I unwilling to negotiate?
- What are my core values, and how are they being defined in my life?
- How do I feel when one of my core values isn't being honored?

Are You a Discounter?

One thing that I have found in my work is that so many of us are quick to discount our previous experience. I hear comments like "No one would ever consider me for this because I've never done that," or "I've never been a manager," or "I've never been someone responsible for money," or "I've never done this or I've never done that." People tend to completely discount everything they've done up to that point in their lives, almost as if it had no relevance.

I experienced this feeling many times myself, especially as I made the transition from musician to salesperson. I would say things to myself like "Why would anyone hire an ex-musician to sell anything?" and "What do I know about business?"

After almost a year of this negative self-talk, I came to understand that sales was, first and foremost, about building relationships and then persuading and convincing people that what you have to offer has value. Think about the musicians that you like and ask yourself if they have built a relationship with you, and if you are convinced that what they create is of any value. I discounted my ability to sell, when in fact I had been in sales for years and didn't even know it.

This type of discounting appears over and over again in the work I do with my clients. I once did some work with a stay-at-home mother who had a college degree. Right out of school she started a family, and now, in her midthirties, she was getting back into the workforce. Her comment to me was "Nobody's going to hire me. What have I done? What experience do I have in business?" I always get a good laugh at comments like that because I look at my wife, who currently owns and runs a small business and had a career in the childcare profession before she decided to stay at home with our kids.

Running a household and raising a family requires executive, midmanagement, and an entire array of competent business skills. You have to be extremely organized, an efficient time manager, a competent planner, a drill sergeant, a psychologist, a mediator, and you must have the ability to negotiate at multiple strategic levels with all age groups and occupations. I've seen many stay-at-home mothers who have spreadsheets upon spreadsheets of information, calendars, journals, and press releases.

As we went through the process, she, like many others, began to realize the vast amount of proven work-related experience she had.

I've discussed this topic extensively with human resources professionals throughout the globe and asked them if it's more important that the person has a master's degree or that they have relevant related experience. More often than not, they would prefer related work experience.

Being a lifelong learner, I'm a huge believer in education and do not disagree that a college degree is an amazing accomplishment. I also realize that there are some professions where advanced degrees are required, but for many exciting positions, including owning your own business, it's not a requirement.

For myself, I would rather have a highly motivated person with related, relevant experience, whether it's in a specific field or another field, than an unmotivated scholar who's never held any type of position or never had the responsibility of accomplishing a real-world task.

The valuable lesson and Quarter Turn to consider is that all experience has value and education, be it in a classroom, library, or anywhere else. This experience increases your understanding and awareness of the world. People who are committed to learning and challenging themselves are generally more satisfied with their own lives and end up accomplishing a great deal that also helps others.

Ask yourself:

- Where am I discounting myself or my previous experience and all the amazing abilities I bring to the table?
- Am I a lifelong learner?
- What education have I achieved outside of the classroom that is relevant to the job I am now holding or pursuing?
- What Quarter Turns have I already made in my life that I am now discounting?

Are You "*Nexting*"?

One of the amazing attributes of the human brain is that it has the ability to project us into the future. Neuroscientists call this "nexting." As far as we are aware, humans are the only creatures on the planet that can think about what will happen next and give ourselves all types of incredible options. This amazing feature allows us to build cities, explore space, create businesses, set big goals, and plan our lives.

One of the challenges of "nexting," especially in this hyperconnected age of digital gadgets, is that we can become so busy thinking about what is next that we actually have difficulty with one of the most basic aspects of humanity, and that is being present' (especially when we are with those we care about the most, or participating in those events that we have looked forward to). The moment we start "nexting," we are no longer fully present.

How many times have you really looked forward to being somewhere, or with someone, and the minute you get there your brain starts to wander off into thinking about what you are going to do next? Being present and in the moment is much harder than you might think.

How often does this happen, and how much are we really cheating ourselves and those around us of these amazing moments in our lives because our brains are constantly thinking about something else? This has a way of destroying our relationships and creating a general sense of unhappiness.

Ask yourself:

- With whom in my life have I decided to be fully present?
- When will the next opportunity come to practice being present?
- How will I plan to just "*be*" with that person and enjoy his/her company?
- What will be the impact on this relationship when I stop "nexting" and start "connecting"?

As you stop nexting and begin to be fully present, notice how many new Quarter Turns become apparent to you.

Are You Listening?

If I were to ask you if you are a good listener, would you say, "Absolutely, I'm a great listener," or, "I'm a pretty good listener"? Those seem to be the most common answers, and yet once we start exploring it and going through the behaviors of a good listener and what that looks like, most people are often shocked and appalled at what a poor listener they have become. And I'm just as guilty as anybody.

We all believe we're such good multitaskers. "Well, I can multitask; I can do more than one thing at a time. . . " Allow me to share something—you cannot multitask. I've never met anyone who can multitask and listen to someone else effectively, and science is beginning to confirm this. The latest studies on the brain are telling us what most already know: we are incapable of concentrating on two things simultaneously. We are more like bumble bees buzzing around from flower to flower. We are not actually multitasking . . . it just doesn't work.

There's a term called "already listening." That's when you run into someone, either in person or on the phone, and you already know exactly what the conversation is going be about and have already made your assumptions and conclusions. It sounds a bit like this: "Uh-huh, OK, yeah, sure, I got it, see ya, bye!" Sound familiar?

Let me ask you this: When you're on the phone with somebody, do you know when he or she is starting to answer his or her e-mails or do some other work? Of course you do, and this person is not even in front of you. And yet, we feel we're so clever. "I'm not listening to this person, but I'm acting like I am."

Let me ask you another question: When you are in a conversation with someone, do you know yourself when you've lost them? Of course you do! So don't think for one minute that you're fooling anybody when they've lost you. You're not. People are perceptive, and they know.

Think about those you come into contact with that are good at listening. They have some very common characteristics: they're typically fully engaged, they're looking at you, and their body language is wide open. Good listeners are focused on you, interested, and *not* multitasking.

Think of the poor listeners now, arms crossed, not even looking at you, unfocused, easily distracted, changing the subject, on their phones, checking e-mails and texts. See the difference?

People who are good listeners ask relevant questions. The questions tend to focus on the topic you were talking about because they are more interested in *you*. It's not all about them and their agenda. When people are genuinely interested in you, they make you feel important. That feels pretty good, doesn't it?

How often are you practicing effective listening skills? If you are like most people these days, then my guess would be very little. Do you wonder why maybe some people aren't all that excited about being around you? Why some of your most important relationships have disintegrated? Do you ever wonder why people aren't engaged or do not buy into some of your ideas or messages? Could it be because you don't pay attention?

Ask yourself:

- Am I listening to those around me, or simply waiting to say what I want to say?
- With whom can I be a better listener, and what will be the impact of doing so?

Becoming an active listener allows us the benefit of learning other people's Quarter Turns and often helps us make sense of our own—all because we are choosing to actually listen.

People Don't Do Things to You

I believe that we all need a good coach in our lives, and I have been fortunate to have many. One of the first coaches to have an impact on me happened to be one of the most amazing women I've ever met . . . my mom.

When I was growing up, she was the principal and chief administrator of an adult education program for the public school system. All throughout my school years I used to visit her after class, mostly because I thought it was cool to be in the principal's office and not be in trouble!

During those years, I used to watch all types of people come into that office really upset. Students would come in upset, parents complaining, teachers freaking out, other administrators angry about one thing or another. I'm telling you, that office could be a very stressful place at times.

No matter what was happening, my mom would play it cool and just listen to each and every person, even as they said nasty things about her or the program. When they finished, she would take a few notes, smile, thank them for sharing their opinions, and then simply go about her business like it never happened. I also noticed that most everyone left that office feeling much better than when they arrived.

One day I finally asked, "Mom, how do you deal with all that, and why would you even want to?" She said something to me that day that has really stuck with me through my entire life. "Tim, I learned a long time ago that when people come into this office and they are really upset, I really don't have anything to do with it. People don't do things to you. They tend to do those things because they are upset about something else; you just happen to be there in front of them at the time."

Later on in my life, one of my favorite colleagues shared with me the statement "people don't do things to you, they do things for themselves." Wow, what a powerful Quarter Turn. As I've gotten older, I've realized this to be true over and over again, and the biggest reason for that is because we are simply not that important to them. Think about it for a minute. People do not wake up in the morning deciding the many ways they plan to ruin our day or get under our skin. They just do things because they are hurt or upset, and we happen to be there when they decide to let it all out.

The challenge is that we tend to take on that negativity as if it's our own, and then we send it right back to them or others that happen to come into our path. Oftentimes we do this to those we care about the most. The worst part is that we can place those people in a drawer and never really allow them to climb their way out, which can have a negative impact on our personal and professional relationships.

Ask yourself:

- Who has "done something" to me that was really doing it for themselves?
- How do I plan to let go of that to begin to build the relationship again?
- Who have I "placed in the drawer" and who am I unwilling to let back into my life or business?
- How much wasted energy and effort have I placed in this relationship because I am unwilling to resolve the situation?

Do People Push Your Buttons?

Are there people that cause you to react in certain ways? People who know how to "push your buttons"? Why do you think they continuously push your buttons? Because they can!

If you don't like the way you react to certain individuals or certain things, change it. Change your interpretation of that event and change the way you behave. When you do something different, you force those around you to do something different.

Let me say that again. When you act or behave differently, people around you are forced to act or behave differently, too. The empowering piece of this is that YOU cause this by the change you bring to the situation. Just feeling differently about people can force them to act differently.

Think about somebody that you know you react negatively to. Now, start thinking differently about this person. Start changing your belief system toward this person. Even if you do nothing differently, just that shift in your belief system will cause a change in that person. It's really amazing. But WHO really does the changing? You do. Isn't that incredible? By doing something different, you create a different outcome.

There is one caveat I must make you aware of that may disappoint you: even when you change your approach or your belief system, and as a result this person acts or behaves differently by that cause and effect, you still may not like what they do. This is where you get to learn and grow. The good news is you have proven that by changing your response or reaction to this person, YOU have caused a change.

As a leader, or in your life, you get to accept the fact that others may not do what you want them to do, but hopefully you've at least proven to yourself one thing: that by doing something different, others will do things differently as well. So if you still don't like the outcome you are getting, you're going to get to do something different once more. It's a chain reaction, but it starts with you and nobody else.

I know what you are saying to yourself right now. "Well you don't know this person, or that person will never do anything different. Why'd this happen, why'd they do that? They should do this, should do that, should, should, should, should!" And then you're "shoulding" all over yourself and everybody else.

The fact is you have no say in how people are going to react and what they're going to do. You only have a say regarding one person, and that's yourself: how you react and what you do. You can control how you feel simply by changing your beliefs around certain events and around certain people.

Ask yourself:

- Who do I know that always seems to push my buttons?
- I already know what they are going to do or say, so what do I plan to do differently the next time it happens?

Pay attention to what this person says or does as a result of your shift in behavior.

It's a big concept, but making this small shift, this one Quarter Turn, can have a huge impact and can actually cause a change in those around you.

Grande Nonfat Latte

I went on my weekly visit to Starbucks to get my usual morning fix and started to wonder just what it was that caused me to spend four or five bucks on such a trivial and non-vital beverage. I decided to stay in the café and finish my drink to ponder this thought. I sat and watched twenty or so devotees come in to order their favorites with all the crazy names and whipped-up concoctions, and then smile while they patiently waited until the barista would call out the name of their liquid addictions. (Almost like an iTunes playlist, I believe there is a future in personality profiling based on a person's Starbucks drink of choice.)

As I sat, sipped, and watched, something occurred to me: Starbucks is a really great place to just be. There is something about how you feel when you are in a Starbucks. The rooms are warm, open, and inviting. The colors are comfortable, the people that work there are almost always in a good mood and happy that you came. Then it finally hit me. Starbucks is not really in the business of selling coffee; Starbucks sells an experience!

I started to think about every time I had ever been to a Starbucks, in all the cities and towns I have visited, even the little hole-in-the-wall shops located at airports and grocery stores, and it all made sense to me. I almost always feel better when I leave a Starbucks than when I get there. That's a pretty big deal in the business world. If I didn't feel good about it, then why would I carry my cup out of the store and bring it with me to wherever I'm going so everyone can see where I've been? In some small way, it's like wearing the "I Voted!" sticker on your shirt on Election Day so you can show everyone what a good citizen of democracy you are.

I have no idea how this coffee store has managed to do this, but I know for a fact that it's the reason why I go there versus some other store for a cheaper blend. When I go to McDonald's for just about anything, I feel worse when I leave than before I get there, so there is something to this. I believe Whole Foods is doing much the same as Starbucks, and I'm certain that Target probably invented the entire concept. Where else can I go in with the intention of buying one small item, leave spending $200, and still feel good about it?

I've realized that although it may seem trivial and self-serving, there is a good feeling I get from going and spending a little too much for a cup of joe. I've also decided that if I can get that much joy out of spending an extra buck or two, well, then so be it. So please excuse me as I'm off to get my fix. "Grande nonfat latte, please!"

Ask yourself:

- What type of experience am I creating for people I come into contact with?
- Do people feel better or worse after they have an interaction with me?
- What are the little pleasures that give me a moment of joy, and am I still doing them for myself?

The Beautiful People

Who are you? Who shows up in the moment?

Do you show up as the right person at the right time, the right person at the wrong time, or the wrong person at the wrong time?

Some of you may remember *Sybil*, the movie about the woman with multiple personality disorder. Don't worry; I am not suggesting you have this condition. However, we all have many different personalities that live within us. Here is a handful that comes to mind:

Dreamer, athlete, competitor, fixer, fighter, romantic, wanderer, guilt monger, realist, pretender, joker, business person, artist, warrior, awfulizer, catastrophizor, caretaker, salesperson, worrier, doubter, skeptic, achiever, driver, risk taker, pusher, blamer, critic, coach, mentor, listener, teacher, student, father, mother, brother, sister, grandmother, grandfather, son, daughter, adult, child, parent . . .

Or any other you can think of.

Learning to call on the right personality at the right time is a strategy that will help you achieve at a higher level.

It's important to remember that these inflections of our personality are a part of us; not honoring any one of them is not being true to our authentic self. Rather than resist when a side of our personality shows up, it's much more productive to simply acknowledge and accept this piece of ourselves, and then get curious about whether it helps or hurts our performance and results.

I've already shared with you that I was a touring musician for many years. There is a creative artist that is still very much a part of who I am. Writing and speaking at conferences and seminars is an outlet that allows me to honor the creative artist in a productive format.

Another part of that musician is the rock and roll rebel. This is the person that challenges authority and resists conforming to other people's rules or the status quo. I really like this person, but he can get me into trouble when he decides to show up at the wrong time, like with my family or in an important meeting with a client. However, if I don't allow him the opportunity to show himself somewhere, like a concert with my friends or at some public gathering, then he's going to show up anyway but probably not in a very productive way.

Your task:

- Go through the list and write down all that apply to you at one time or another (feel free to add any of your own that are not on the list).
- Once you have identified all that are part of you, decide which two you value the most and which two you value the least and write out why.
- Once you have explored those, decide which of these personalities tends to show up at the right place but the wrong time and probably get you a result that you are not looking for.
- Extra credit if you decide on a strategy to deal with that personality when he or she decides to show up at the wrong time!

Now that you have taken the first steps to become aware of who you are and how you show up, it is time to take that next big Quarter Turn and gain some clarity on what it is you actually want.

Section 2

Clarity

What exactly do you want in your life, your business, and your relationships? Simple questions, right? Surprisingly, very few people can answer those questions with extreme clarity or definition. Often we skirt around the question by saying things like "Well, I kinda want this . . . maybe if I did that . . . wouldn't it be great if I had this . . . I wish I could be that." Sound familiar? Gaining extreme clarity on the things you want in your life and defining exactly what that looks like seems to be the hardest part in actually obtaining them.

Think about what you want for a minute. Once you get past the obvious things like more money, a bigger house, or an exotic car, ask yourself again what it is you really want. Can you describe it with any detail? Do you see yourself doing or having what you just described? This is the first step toward believing it's actually possible.

Napoleon Hill wrote, "What the mind of a man can conceive and believe, it can achieve." The hardest part of that equation from my experience is usually the conceiving part, followed closely by the believing part. Our minds have an amazing way of moving us toward those things that we focus on with extreme clarity. Once the destination is clear, the path to get there doesn't seem so daunting. These next Quarter Turns are designed to help you gain some of that clarity and give you what you need to fine-tune what you want in your life.

What is Your Vision?

One of the big separators of super high achievers and everybody else is an amazing sense of clarity and vision. Read any book or watch an interview about a highly successful person, and the common denominator is they always just knew exactly what they wanted and where they were going. They all faced challenges and obstacles along the way, but they never allowed those setbacks to throw them off their path and vision. Even in the face of negativity and people that told them they could never do what they said they wanted to do, somehow these individuals were able to stay the course and just keep moving forward.

Did you know that Michael Jordan, arguably the best basketball player of all time, did not make the varsity squad for his high school basketball team as a sophomore, and he ended up being the greatest JV player of all time? Who cuts Michael Jordan from any team? Walt Disney was fired from a local newspaper because he was told he "lacked imagination." REALLY? Decca Records didn't offer the Beatles a record contract because they were told "guitar music was on the way out"! The Beatles! The list goes on and on, but the message is loud and clear: clarity and vision about exactly what you want internally and the mental fortitude to keep pushing forward are much more important than external forces buying in.

Effective people and leaders have a clear vision of where they are going and clearly communicate a consistent vision for themselves and their organizations, even in the face of adversity.

Ask yourself:

- If my team or those around me were asked about my vision, what would they say?
- What is my vision for me and for my team?
- How am I communicating this vision?

- How am I handling the naysayers or the negativity around my vision?
- Where can I make improvements in the conveyance of my vision to create buy-in and help motivate my team?
- What will be the impact on me or my organization if I achieve my vision?

Belief of Knowing What It Is You Want

One of the most interesting things about clarity and how it actually works is learning to identify and embrace all of the times in your life you have actually attained something you were extremely clear about and wanted badly enough, only to have it show up in a different way than you had envisioned it.

Your job is to think about and focus intently on some really great "whats" you want in your life. Really stretch yourself, and, for the time being, don't worry about the "how." The way that the "how" presents itself to you will sometimes surprise you, and many times you may not even recognize that you have achieved it, because it comes in such a radically different package. I will share with you the best way that this has happened to me in my life.

As I alluded to earlier, in my teenage years and through most of my twenties I was in a fairly successful rock and roll band. We never got signed, so you have never heard of us, but regionally we did pretty well for ourselves. We toured the country, opened up for very large acts, played arenas, recorded an album, had our songs played on popular radio stations, won contests, and also went overseas and played in Russia, of all places. Clearly, that was what I thought I was going to do with my life. I thought my purpose was to be a singer in a rock and roll band.

The goal was always very clear to me: get signed by a major label, release an album, get on MTV, and sell millions of records, done deal! That was the path back in the days before we had the Internet, YouTube, and iTunes. Back then, getting on MTV was the sign that you made it, and MTV, for those of you who are too young to remember, actually used to play music videos, so I've totally dated myself.

As I previously mentioned, our band's success was short-lived, and we became a victim of the changing musical climate of the early '90s. The switch over to grunge music was ultimately our undoing, and a huge Quarter Turn that I learned in that moment was that "timing is everything."

It didn't really matter how good we were or how talented we were, musical tastes had shifted, and the type of music we were playing wasn't going to allow us to be successful in the "new normal" (a valuable lesson for any business).

From an early age, I had always believed that I could accomplish anything I wanted if I focused and worked hard enough, but for whatever reason, being in a band wasn't working. I was really depressed for a while, and I went into what I call the "dark days," but I emerged from that. I finished up my degree and got into sales.

My rapid success in the sales organization caused the leadership to ask me if I would be interested in conducting sales trainings in front of the entire company. As I shared earlier, somehow I had discovered a path to get back to doing exactly what I loved doing the most: getting up in front of an audience and having an impact on them, and maybe causing them to feel just a little bit better than when they showed up.

Soon I was asked to speak at larger local and regional conferences, and for a performer, the bigger the audience, the better. Around this time, I got the call from my sister Ann who had just started a small training and HR consulting company in Las Vegas, and you know the rest of the story. Here is where it gets interesting.

One of our first clients happened to be Palms Casino Resort in Las Vegas, who wanted us to conduct training and development for its opening. After the opening, the resort was doing a television program called *Real World Las Vegas* for MTV. The owners loved the work that we did so much that they asked us to come in and be part of the program and do some of our training with the kids on the show. My sister wasn't sure if we should do it and wasn't really even sure exactly what *Real World* was all about, but she knew it was on MTV and wanted to ask me about it. After we discussed exactly what we were being tasked with, we agreed that it was good for the business and told them we would do it.

I remember thinking, as we were filming the first day the kids showed up, how interesting it was to see exactly how they film these types of shows.

Early on that first day of filming, one of the kids caused a scene and walked out of the room. I later learned that's how the people on reality shows get screen time—by creating little dramas.

The producers knew I was a business coach and asked me to go out and convince the person to come back and join the group. So I followed him. I found him, and we started to have a conversation. Suddenly all of the cameras were upon us, and I thought, "Whoa boys, back up a bit" since it was a little awkward having a rather large camera jammed right into your face. Surprisingly after a few minutes I got used to it and didn't mind all the cameras. The young reality star and I talked for a while. I did a bit of coaching to help him through his situation, and finally he agreed to come back to join the group.

As we walked back and the cameras shut down and moved away, I thought to myself, "That little piece might actually get on the show." Right at that second it hit me like a ton of bricks! I just got on MTV—I had finally made it! I had gotten to a place that for so long was such a big goal of mine. The interesting part about it was that it wasn't at all how I thought I would get there.

Now it took a second, and I almost didn't realize it when it happened because it didn't show up in the form that I thought it would. I believed that I was going to get onto MTV playing music with a guitar and a mic, but that's not how it happened. I got there a completely different way than I ever could have imagined back in my early twenties, but I got there.

Now to extrapolate this concept even further, as I started digging into this years later, through my coaching and through the work I do with my own personal coaches, I started asking myself about that one big goal that I didn't achieve. I never got a record contract, and I never did all of those things that I thought I was going to do, but I asked myself what was it that I loved so much about music—why is it that I wanted to be in a band in the first place?

As I started answering those questions, the first thing that I realized is that I love to perform in front of a group of people and have an impact. It is the thing I love most in the world next to my family and my kids. I love performing. You can put two people in front of me, two thousand people in front of me, or twenty thousand people in front on me; if there is an audience, then I am at home.

In addition, one of the things that I thought would be great about being in a successful band is that I would get to travel all over the place and stay at exotic resorts and meet really incredible people. Well, if you think about what I do for a living now, I perform in front of groups small and large all over the world. I travel more than I would care to travel (be careful what you wish for is the lesson there!), and I meet really great people that work for or run amazing companies. So all of the things that I wanted, well, I got them. They just didn't show up in the way that I thought they would.

I thought my goals and dreams would be realized with a guitar and a microphone. I still have a microphone, I am just not singing and playing guitar.

On a side note, just recently I released some songs independently on iTunes. I have no idea how many downloads we have, because that's not what matters to me. What matters is that I was able to get a record released and do those things I wanted to do.

When it comes to clarity, ask yourself:

- What are those things I want?

Avoid getting caught up in the details of how you are going to get that, or how you are going to do that. Just put it out there for now. Let the universe conspire to put the pieces into place.

If it's clear what you want, if it's important enough, and if you focus enough energy in that direction, then it will happen.

More importantly, when it happens, don't miss it, because it's not likely to come in the package you expect.

Rocks of All Shapes and Sizes

The "rocks" in your life represent the most important and valuable things you already do (or want to do), see, have, or experience. Identifying what these are can offer you guidance and clarity each and every day, and cause you to make decisions that will bring you greater joy and happiness. Follow the process below and create the "rocks" in your journey.

Write this down:

- **Skipping Stones** – These are the simple things that can be done daily or whenever you like. They usually cost little or nothing, but they give you an immense amount of joy and satisfaction—a hug from a loved one, tossing the ball, playing the piano, a nice glass of wine, watching your favorite TV program, playing a board game, phoning a friend, the first cup of coffee in the morning, sleeping in! Simple, easy, and enjoyable. List twenty-five or more Skipping Stones.
- **Stepping Stones** – These are bigger things and usually require a bit more planning and effort compared to simple things—dinner out with friends, attending a concert, watching a loved one's sporting event, purchasing a new outfit, going to the movies, detailing your car, having a garage sale, sleeping in (again)! These are not seismic events in your life; nonetheless, they are sources of joy

and excitement and can be done weekly or monthly with a bit of effort. List twenty-five or more Stepping Stones.

- **Flag Stones** – These are important events that do not happen every day—wedding anniversaries, birthdays (yours or anyone else's), holiday traditions, a family vacation to Florida, a weekend jaunt to the slopes, new cars, new homes, new jobs. These usually involve greater effort and resources to plan and execute. List twenty-five or more Flag Stones.

- **Big Rocks** – These are dreams and lifelong goals of yours. No limits, no boundaries—standing on the Great Wall of China, wandering the Roman ruins, sailing the Greek islands, a home on the ocean, the dream car you have always wanted, owning your home free and clear, a college diploma, masters degree, or doctorate. These are things that truly inspire you and typically involve the greatest degree of effort and resources to execute. List twenty-five or more Big Rocks.

All of the items in the above lists should be personal and unique to you. Also, no one else should have input on your selections—this is your list. Remember: twenty-five of each is the bare minimum. You can write as many as you allow your heart to open to! Add your "rocks" to your journal and watch how many Quarter Turns come as a result.

Time Affluence

If you ask most people in the world what would make them happy, I'm sure just about everyone would tell you, "More money." To some extent, they would be absolutely right. Yet some of the latest data on health, happiness, and general well-being is confirming something that many of us have already found out: money doesn't equate to happiness.

It is true that until basic needs are met (food, shelter, etc.), money really can "buy" happiness. But once basic needs are met, the latest studies tell us that those with more money are really no happier or more content than those with less.

So what, then, is the great separator that makes some so much happier than others? Clearly there are some genetic predispositions that we can take into account, but again, most of us are not clinically depressed and don't have hormone deficiencies that may cause us to be less happy than our neighbors. The data is telling us something really amazing in that how we spend our time makes all the difference.

Taken literally, what this means is that your future happiness is not dependent upon how much money you make, but how and with whom you choose to spend your most valuable commodity: time. Think about it—with all of our communication devices and social networks, we should feel more connected, yet overall happiness has actually gone down, and people are describing themselves as feeling more alone.

A recent study of young mothers found that many didn't actually enjoy the time they spend with their children . . . really! It's not that they don't love their children; in fact, most surveyed said their kids were the most important things in their lives. It's the constant shuffling of them from event to event—sports, schools, friends' parties—all the while multitasking on their smartphones with work or friends that created a lot of stress and unhappiness.

Conversely, it's those who took time to slow down and enjoy simple moments (like a quiet meal with their kids, an afternoon in the park, playing a game, or working on an art or craft project) who were quite content and happy with their lives.

Time is the great equalizer. No one gets more or less time, and we can't buy more when our time is up. Time affluence is the currency of the future—are you taking time to savor the moment, or are you thinking about what's next?

This week, take time every day to enjoy a simple pleasure in your life. Call an old friend, sit down and actually taste your food, go to your favorite café, have a real conversation with your spouse or significant other, visit your kid's school. Wherever you are this week . . . BE THERE.

Ask yourself:

- How and with whom am I spending my time?
- Is this a smart use of my most valuable commodity?
- What am I going to do to start using my time in a way that I intend?
- How much of my valuable time is being spent with people and in places that add no value to my life? What am I going to do about it?

It's Not about Me

Being the youngest of six kids in a large Italian family certainly has its perks. As long as I was in the room, it was very rare that I had to do very much. I only had to stand there long enough and look bewildered or look like I needed help, and BOOM! Things got done for me.

That continued throughout my life. I don't know if I consciously sought out people that would take care of things for me, or maybe I just looked like someone who needed people to do things for me. I'm certainly not complaining about it, that's for sure.

However, I did realize at a certain point in my life that maybe this had held me back from doing some of the things that I really wanted to do or experiencing life at an entirely different level. My behavior was causing me to get outcomes that I really did not want for myself.

My whole life I had always felt like it was' about me! It was' always about me. And I suppose I looked for people that supported me in my quest to make everything all about me as well. You know—friends, girlfriends, coworkers, everyone I did business with and seemingly everyone I came into contact with. I wanted everything to be all about me.

Getting married was one of my first realizations that making things all about me can get very old, and that making things all about someone that you care about can be extremely rewarding. I can't believe how long I missed out on this type of satisfaction.

This sense of fulfillment, in committing to being there completely for someone else, came full circle with the birth of my son. I remember looking down at him—his eyes were closed, as he had just been born. He couldn't have been more than a few minutes old. At that moment he looked up at me, his eyes opened just a sliver and he gave me this little smile. WOW, that was a pretty powerful moment for me. It was in that moment that I fully realized, *You know what? It's not all about me*. And it never really has been.

A few years later I was blessed with another son and experienced that same moment all over again. I was reminded that it's about him and not just in that sense of the word, but that I had to take that Quarter Turn into other parts of my life. It's not about me in my relationship with my wife. It's not about me as the youngest in the family with four sisters, two brothers, and four more stepsiblings. It's not about me in my business or in the workplace. It's not always about me with my friends.

This was such a powerful recognition for me, especially when I thought about all of those years that I wasted so much energy in my attempts to make everything all about me. I still have to remember that—because going in and grandstanding and making it about me was a hard habit for me to break.

There are still times that I have to remind myself, "Wait a second; this situation is not about me," "I really have nothing to do with this," "This moment is about or for someone else," or "This is about the person with me right now. I'm here for that person."

Ask yourself:

- Am I making this situation all about me?
- How is that impacting those around me?
- Where am I going to start making things about the people in my life I care about the most?
- What type of person would I like to be?

Making this Quarter Turn has allowed me to become a better person by being someone that can be relied upon by others. If it's always about you, nobody can rely on you. As a leader, and in your life, when those around you can rely on you, watch how your relationships grow to a deep and meaningful level.

In the Zone

All of us have a unique ability, something that, when executed, life seems to flow with effortless ease. When we're performing this unique ability (which oftentimes will occur unconsciously because it's so natural), we are in complete alignment with our purpose. We don't worry about the future, and we think nothing of the past. We are entirely in the moment. Some call it your "sweet spot"; I call it "in the zone."

When I'm in front of a large audience, time seems to stand still for me. I get a real sense of calm and easiness that allows me to operate at a completely different level. Athletes and entertainers talk about this same heightened sense of awareness during competition and performances.

I remember once watching Michael Jordon hit six three-pointers in one quarter of a playoff game, and after he hit the sixth one, he just looked right at the camera, put his hands up, and had this funny look on his face as if to say, "I have no idea how this is happening, but it's pretty cool, right?" He was definitely "in the zone," and he knew it.

You have this same sense as well.

The Quarter Turn is to discover when you are "in the zone." What is that thing that you love to do, that is easy for you to do, that is your natural talent? Ask everyone who knows you (or at least as many people as possible,) what they think your sweet spot is or when they sense that you are "in the zone." You may want to enlist the help of those around you or launch an Internet campaign to accomplish this. Write down what each person says. See if there are similarities or themes among the responses you receive, ask yourself if their assessments resonate with you.

Were you surprised by what you heard? Did any of the feedback illuminate some of your natural talents? What do you think your sweet spot is? When do you feel "in the zone"? Are the people you asked right? Is there something else that lights you up that they might not know about? Where do you currently apply your natural talent and ability? At home? At work? Somewhere else? Where can it be applied more?

Identifying this Quarter Turn is an important step if we would ever like to gain the type of clarity that allows us to perform at higher levels. When we focus on our true gifts, we are focusing on doing something that brings us incredible happiness and joy because it is intrinsically what we love and are meant to do.

- When are you "in the zone"?
- When are you going to be there next?

The Other Side

Many people put a great deal of emphasis on the quality of their professional life. More often than not, two strangers get to know each other by starting with the topic of what they do for a living. It is not until much further in the conversation that people share what they are interested in that has nothing to do with their career. Often success in the workplace is interpreted as success in life and serves to justify any consideration to all of the other facets of our lives.

One side of our life is work and the other side is everything else, but the work side is what gets most, if not all, of our attention. That other side of our lives that we tend to neglect oh, so often and put off till tomorrow is the side we want to focus on. In doing so, you might see that improving that "other side" will also benefit the side you might think needs all of your attention.

There are people that I work with that are struggling in relationships with their husband, wife, significant other, kids, family members, or whomever. It seems as though all of their efforts to improve the relationship fall flat. I usually ask them, "If this person in your life that you want to build a relationship with were a business or a company that you work for and you were going to the board of directors, would you be getting a raise? Would you be getting a lateral move, or would you be getting fired?" When I present it that way, for many people, it's like getting hit in the face by a two-by-four. They often will say, "You know what, Tim? I'd probably be getting fired, or at least put on a performance plan." It's then I ask if it's any wonder they're having trouble with this relationship.

If you think about your business and your workplace, think of all the planning you do. You schedule meetings, you' have strategic planning sessions, you' meet two weeks later to make sure you are following the plan, you' meet two weeks after that to decide if that plan is the plan you want to stay on, and then you' have another meeting to plan for the next strategic planning meeting, and so on and so forth. You have countless measuring tools to see how you're doing—you're looking at your profit and loss statements, you're looking at your invoices, and you're looking at your monthly billing cycle. You know exactly where you're at all the time.

Some will attend seminars about communicating with coworkers and people in their workplace, facilitating, conflict management, and leadership, and so many other topics designed to improve the workplace.

When was the last time you had a strategic planning meeting with your spouse? When was the last time you had a family planning session on things you wanted to do over the summer? When's the last time you measured to see if you were hitting the mark? When's the last time you attended a seminar not based around business in order to learn something about the other side?

Do you realize how little time and effort you spend on the people that you say are the most important to you? If you're not happy with the relationship that you have with someone, ask yourself what you've done to improve it, other than say, "Well, you know, I made a phone call!" So what? What have you really done? Have you gotten in there and really decided it's important to you? Have you made the time or made the appointment with yourself?

A lesson I had to learn long ago was that if I didn't put the kids' events and the things that were important to me on my calendar, I wouldn't do them. So now when a client says, "I have time on this day to meet," if it happens to fall on a time reserved for family, I tell them, "You know what? I already have an appointment scheduled then, how about this time or that time?" I don't necessarily let them know that it's my son's soccer game or a family event. If they asked I certainly would tell them, but nobody ever asks. They say, "Well how about this other date?"

I see people cancelling those "non-work" appointments so often, but they would never cancel an appointment with a client, customer, or coworker. How quick we are to say that's not important. I've heard it said many times that on their death bed, nobody ever wished they had spent more time at the office, more time at work, or sent just one more e-mail.

The one thing I know about my family, particularly my two boys, is that at some point they're not going to want to spend time with me. They're going to be off doing their own things, and I'm going to be the one saying, "Hey, can I?" or "Are you available?" and "Do you want to?" And the response will be "No, I'm too busy, Dad" or "Go ahead without me." I know that day is coming soon, so I don't want to miss anything now.

Are you taking the time and putting in the effort so that when you do go in that boardroom to get evaluated on how your business is doing with the most important people in your life, you're not going to get fired, you're not going to get a lateral move? You are absolutely getting a promotion and a big fat raise with the bonus! Start today!

Goal Setting

There are many books, software packages, and ideas about goal setting, but from my experience the most common reason people don't achieve their goals is simply because they don't have any. Isn't that interesting? They just don't have any. They think about them sometimes in their head and this is how they commit. "Boy, wouldn't it be great if I did that? Wouldn't it be nice if I did this?" But there's nothing that's concrete, and there is very little commitment.

I've gotten into the habit of constantly writing down goals. Sometimes they're as simple as getting the door fixed at the house, and sometimes they're as big as starting a college fund and contributing a certain amount of money for my kids' education. It doesn't really matter what the goals are, the most important thing to do is actually write them down. I coach this simple exercise to no end. Write down your goals!

There is something about writing goals down that causes them to happen. I learned this from my first business coach, Bob. He used to always say, "Write them down. Write down your goals. Write down twelve personal and twelve professional goals, and then put a time frame on it."

The act of writing something down seems to force our mind to focus on a specific idea, which seems to help compel the rest of us to make it happen. I like to take a few moments in the morning and jot down my goals for the day and to review my progress on goals I have already committed to paper. This seems to set the tone for how I move forward after my morning coffee. When I get too far away from this simple process, I tend to drift and become unfocused. Consequently, I feel as though I'm not accomplishing anything, and that starts an entire stress-driven dialogue in my head, which is extremely unproductive. Sound familiar to anyone? Commit to starting a habit or writing out those goals—big and small—that are important to you.

Start today by writing out twelve personal and twelve professional goals!

The Science of Goal Setting

Documenting your goals provides clarity and purpose. We all talk about goals and things we are committed to, but very rarely do we take the time to document them. The mere fact of going through this exercise causes us to get clear and specific on what we actually want.

Don't worry if you've found this exercise to be challenging, as many people struggle with this seemingly simple exercise. Regardless of what level of achievement we have accomplished, most of us haven't trained our minds to get this specific and clear on exactly what we want. Many people go through life not ever knowing what it is they truly desire. On the other hand, I've found that almost everyone seems to be extremely clear on what they DON'T want, and that becomes a habit as well.

As we write goals out, we start to decide if they are really what we want, or perhaps learn they are things we thought we wanted, or used to want, but no longer have any relevance in our lives. What an awesome realization! This clarity oftentimes relieves us of incredible stress, because consciously we were telling ourselves we wanted something, when in actuality the want was not in line with what we truly value.

This uncertainty creates a constant push and pull, creating an underlying tension, which in turn short-circuits the goal, causing us to never fully commit, and consequently we fail to achieve a goal we were never really committed to. The reward for this is that we then get to beat ourselves up and feel bad because we didn't accomplish what we said we were going to do. This vicious cycle repeats itself over and over, until we finally refuse to set any meaningful goals at all. Sound familiar?

Once we have the goal documented, we can begin to look at the goal objectively and with fresh eyes; it's no longer this deep, dark mystery. It's now real and something that can be mapped out systematically and logically like any task.

Because documenting a goal seems to bring life to it, we give ourselves the opportunity to truly believe that the goal is possible;

many times we shut ourselves down in the belief phase, which is another reason why we never write the goal down in the first place. Think about it: How are we ever supposed to accomplish anything amazing if we don't even know what we actually want? Clarity is the key.

So, if you've found yourself struggling, not to worry: just keep going. Take each goal one at a time, and focus on getting specific and clear. And remember, this is one of the greatest gifts you can ever give yourself. And if you did the entire exercise in one sitting, don't stop at twenty-four goals! Write down as many as you can think of!

Goals Finale

Read any book or article about highly successful people and you will find a common denominator: they all have clear goals and are highly focused on exactly what they want.

As I just mentioned, most of us tend to focus on just the opposite, which is what we don't want. The problem with that type of thinking is that your brain goes after what you choose to focus on, kind of like a GPS mapping system except it doesn't recognize "do" or "don't," only "where." So make sure you are plugging in the correct destination.

Once you program in the coordinates, your brain automatically takes you in that direction even in the unconscious state. So once you are focused on what you want, write it down, and get extreme clarity on the goal, you will automatically start moving toward it.

I'll prove it to you. Have you ever heard a great song on the radio driving home—and man, do you love that song—but for the life of you, you can't remember who the artist is? You think and think, and stress and even ask a few friends, but just can't remember. Finally you just give up. Then one or two days later, in the middle of lunch with a friend or a colleague, you just blurt out, "DEF LEPPARD!"

Everyone has had that happen at one point or another. Maybe you went to bed with a big, complex problem that you couldn't solve and then in the morning you magically woke up with the perfect solution. In both of these situations you were not consciously searching for the answer, but somehow you got to it. That's the magic of clear, concise goals. Once you have them programmed into the system, your brain just sort of moves you in that direction whether you want to or not.

Making this one Quarter Turn of having clarity and focus on what you want instead of what you don't want is a huge step, and ultimately will help you identify and overcome the obstacles that can get in your way.

Section 3

Obstacles

My first business coach once said to me, "Life hands you the same lesson over and over again until you figure out how you are going to deal with it!" I've since added that life will also hand you the same type of people over and over again until you figure out how you are going to learn to relate to or communicate with them as well.

In my coaching practice, much of the time spent with clients is helping them uncover and identify those obstacles that have prevented them from achieving at a high level. What are the barriers that have caused us to remain stuck in the same place, in our lives, in our businesses, and in those relationships that mean so much to us? Going through this process helps remove the mystery around why we aren't making progress. Oftentimes there is an internal struggle going on, and we are uncertain of the cause.

Clearly identifying these obstacles and barriers allows us to put the problem front and center. Being able to identify the challenge or problem allows the solution to become much more apparent and less daunting to us. At the very least, we can now put a name to this "Big Bad Wolf" and start calling it what it is, instead of what it isn't.

We will all encounter obstacles along the path to our goals, so now it's time to clearly identify exactly what yours are. You know because you have lived with them for so long and probably used them as an excuse to not move forward in the direction you wish to go. Now that you have some awareness and clarity, it's time to explore these obstacles and start clearing the path toward your new destinations, one Quarter Turn at a time.

The Baseball Bat

When my son Dylan was ten, he started playing on a competitive baseball team. In our area they call it "Travel Ball." He's a pretty good little baseball player, loves to play. He loves all sports, but like his father seemed to have a real love for playing baseball.

At the start of the season, Dylan was having some trouble hitting the ball. For some reason, he just wasn't making good contact. He's got a great swing and up to that point was a pretty good hitter, so he was experiencing his first slump. As anyone can attest to, it's easy to get down on yourself when you aren't performing as well as you know you can. Dylan is a pretty intense little athlete, so he was really getting down on himself.

I kept asking him what he thought was going on. "Well, I can't hit the ball . . . can't hit the ball . . . I can't do it. I'm so frustrated. It's not working. I can't do it." He was completely stressing himself out about it, and it became a self-fulfilling prophecy. "I can't hit the ball. I can't hit the ball."

While I'm fully aware that what you say to yourself internally is the reality you will get externally, I wasn't sure if Dylan was ready for this type of a concept. So instead Dylan and I started talking about it, and I asked him, "Well, what's going on? What do you think the problem is?" And for a while he said, "I don't know" or "I just can't figure it out." I kept digging with him for a while, until finally he said, "I don't think I like any of the bats we have."

To this, I asked him what he meant that he didn't like any of the bats. "Well, it's too heavy and it's too long!"

I asked him if he was sure about this, and he responded with enthusiasm, "Yeah, that's it!" Finally, after answering a few more of my questions, he was convinced it was the bat. When I looked at him, I could see his energy change as this enormous weight seemed to be lifted off his shoulders. He now knew exactly what his problem was and he was determined to fix it.

Noticing his physical response, I said, "Great, if that's what it is, then why don't we go to the sporting goods store this afternoon and pick out a new bat!" I then added, "But if you get this bat, I want you to promise me you're going to use it. And then you're going to start hitting the ball hard like you have done before." He immediately replied, "Oh yes, no doubt in my mind."

Later that day, we went to the store and started messing around with a few bats. We were there at least two or three hours. I'm sure we looked at and tested just about every single bat in the store, and finally he smiled, looked directly at me, and confidently stated, "Dad, this bat is the one. This bat is the bat, I know it." To which I asked him, "Are you sure?"

We went back and forth on it because it was the most expensive bat in the store, but I made him convince me that this was the bat. Dylan had to sell this to me. He went on and on saying, "This is the one. It feels right. It's got the right size grip for my hands. It swings perfectly; it's everything I've ever wanted in a bat. I want this bat! I have to have this bat!" He was really excited about it and finally convinced me to get him the bat.

Now, clearly I didn't believe the bat was the problem, but Dylan did. He believed that this was the challenge, and he believed that he had found the solution. It doesn't matter if it made any sense or if I believed it was the solution or not, only that he did. If you believe something to be true, then guess what? It's absolutely 100 percent true. It doesn't matter what evidence is there to support it, it doesn't matter if it's right or wrong. What matters is that you decide that this is it.

So, lo and behold, the first time he steps up to the plate with his new bat . . . crack! Base hit right up the middle. From that point on, for the rest of the season, he had no problems hitting a ball.

Now, I know it's kind of a trivial story, and it sounds kind of silly, but ask yourself where in your life you tell yourself that this is your problem. "I have this problem, and there is nothing I can do about it. This is it." And how often is that a self-fulfilling prophecy? How often does that problem come to you over and over and over again?

If you believe it to be true, then it will be true. There is a term called the placebo effect, which is often used in the pharmaceutical industry to assess the true efficiency of a new drug. One group of people will receive the actual drug and the other group will receive a placebo—nothing, sugar water. The researchers tell them that it's the new drug, that it's going to work, and the results can sometimes be fascinating. There are numerous instances where the results were as good with the placebo as with the actual drug.

The power of belief is one of the crucial factors when it comes to solving challenges or problems. You have to believe it is possible first. Then you have to believe that you actually have the answer.

Ask yourself:

- What have I decided are the barriers to success in my life?
- Are they real or did I create them on my own?
- Where do I just need to find a new bat?
- Sometimes a Quarter Turn is just that simple.

Triggers

The most successful people I have ever met know one thing for certain: they are not perfect!

I know what you are thinking, and NO, you are not perfect either. :-)

These individuals also realize they often act or react in a manner that is inconsistent with who they are or where they want to go. What separates these high performing individuals from the rest of the pack is that when they do not achieve the outcomes they desire, they usually don't blame others. Instead they will choose to ask why their own actions didn't get them the outcome they were looking for and what they would do differently if confronted with the same situation again.

In my experience, here are the questions they ask themselves when scrutinizing their actions and behavior:

- What happened?
- How did I respond when it happened?
- How would I like to respond in the future?
- What is the lesson I am supposed to learn from this?
- How will I apply this in the future?

This week, when you feel yourself losing control, I would like for you to focus on the question, "What happened?" The answers to this question typically identify what "set you off" to begin with. What caused you to act or react in a way that is out of alignment with your core values? I refer to these as triggers.

Triggers can be anything: people, places, things, words, emotions, events, or states of being such as hungry, exhausted, or tired. Triggers can be specific or global, but they are very unique to you.

Highly emotionally intelligent people have developed amazing coping skills and mechanisms to deal with these triggers that have challenged them through the years.

Once you identity your triggers, you can take the mystery out of them—and more importantly take control of your future by developing a strategy to deal with your triggers when confronted with them.

Ask yourself:

- What is it that sets me off?
- What are my triggers?
- What causes me to act or react in a manner that is inconsistent with who I am, based on my core values and who I want to become?

Once you've identified your triggers, you can now start applying a few Quarter Turns and learn to effectively deal with them.

Superimposing

I've learned so much in my coaching business over the years and worked with thousands of successful business people that constantly challenge me and force me to "up my game." Many of the Quarter Turns I shared with you are direct results of coaching conversations and discussions that take place in various workshops and seminars that I lead across the globe.

Of all the lessons and Quarter Turns that have shown up in these discussions, there is one that just seems to appear over and over again. I believe this particular lesson is one of the biggest stumbling blocks and obstacles to success in leadership and in life, and one that I'm sure you can relate to. I call it "superimposing."

The very definition of the term is to overlay one thing onto another. Photographers use superimposing to blend two images together and create some interesting shots.

One of the biggest challenges we face in our lives is when we superimpose our own values and beliefs, and the way we would do something onto others. Then, when that person doesn't live up to those values and beliefs or does things differently . . . well, guess how we feel about those people? That's right; it's okay, I already know what you are thinking. We wonder what the heck is wrong with them. Why don't they get it?

In our lives, superimposing might sound like this:

- *"You should know better . . . "*
- *"When I was your age, I was already doing this . . . "*
- *"You should be more like . . . "*

In our business, superimposing sounds like this:

- *"You've worked here for a year, you should be able to . . . "*
- *"This person is a VP of the company; they should . . . "*

- *"This person ought to . . . "*

In our relationships, superimposing might sound like this:

- *"I've done this for you, so you should . . . "*
- *"Why don't you ever . . . "*
- *"You never do . . . "*

Do any of these phrases sound familiar? Notice how often the word *should* is used.

You should do this, you should do that, should, should, should. Basically you are shoulding all over yourself!

Sounds a bit ridiculous, doesn't it? But I bet you can think of a circumstance just this past week when you caught yourself superimposing your own values and beliefs onto someone else.

Let me ask you a question: Is it rational to believe that someone will have the exact same values and beliefs that you have? That someone will learn at the same pace and in the same way that you did? That someone will act and behave just like you do? Of course not! Yet, even though logically we know this doesn't make sense, we still superimpose what we believe to be right on everyone else, don't we? Let me ask you one more question: How's that working for you?

Ask yourself:

- Where am I superimposing my own values and beliefs onto someone else?
- How does that make this person feel? How does it make me feel?
- Am I willing to allow this person to learn and grow in their own way and at their own pace, or does it have to be my way or the highway?

Stress

Stress is inevitable—everyone's going to have a certain amount of it in his/her life. It's impossible to live a life completely stress-free. It seems to me that something that is inevitable might be something that actually helps us if we handle it the right way. Think about it for a moment. How can a natural part of living be a totally destructive force? The answer lies in understanding and moderation.

There are two types of stress. There's distress, which is where you're so stressed, you're frustrated, you're anxious, and you can't do anything. But then there's what they call eustress, which is that amount of stress that sort of tightens the straps a little bit.

Think of it like a fan belt on a car. If the fan belt is too loose, meaning that you just have no stress whatsoever (you're bored out of your mind), how well does the car run? It doesn't run at all. It's slipping. It gets all messed up. It just doesn't work. If the fan belt is too tight (you're completely distressed all the time), what happens to the car? You know, the fan belt eventually snaps and the car doesn't work. The ideal amount of stress is that amount of stress that causes you to perform at an acceptable level, or at optimum performance like the fan belt. If it's at just the right tension, then things work correctly.

What causes some people stress isn't necessarily a stressor for others, so stress can be extremely difficult to gauge, look at, or even talk about. I listen to athletes talk about how they've been playing for years, and they still get those butterflies in their stomach before a game. But they think that's a good thing, and of course it is. I've talked to entertainers that say the same thing. They perform for years, and they still get a few jitters before the big show. I've performed in public now going on twenty-five years, and to this day, before my classes, before my sessions, before my seminars, before I get up in front of a group, I still get a few butterflies. And to me, that's a good thing. I've always said that the day I don't have those is the day I'll probably quit, because that means I just don't care anymore. So there's nothing wrong with a little bit of stress and having some will help you work at an optimum performance level.

There are times when the origin and level of stress is within our control to either reduce it to a manageable level or eliminate it completely. In both my personal and professional experience, I have come to understand that the extent to which a person is experiencing stress is rarely attributed to a single stressor but is the aggregation of multiple stress triggers. Take the time to look at what's causing you stress. Is it work? Is it family? Is it personal? Is it other things? What's happening?

I have countless examples of little stressful things that have added up to become a big stressful event. I suspect that as you are reading this, memories of your own are coming to the forefront that are as relevant as any anecdote I might have. But this book is about little changes we can make in our lives that will improve our lives and the lives of those around us.

Ask yourself:

- What are three things in my life that I believe cause me stress?
- What are three things about each of the things I just listed that I believe make them stressful?
- For each of the nine things that I believe make my life stressful, what is just one strategy I could utilize to either avoid it altogether or allow myself to view this stressor in a way that would no longer be stressful?

Remember, these little Quarter Turns can help to eliminate big stressful events.

Good 'Nuff

My ninth grade baseball coach was named Mr. Dick. No joke, that was his real name. You can imagine how this man was talked about by thousands of adolescent boys and girls, but that is a whole different chapter or book. Mr. Dick was probably the best sports coach I ever had in my life. He was a big man and very intimidating. Rarely did he have kind a word for anyone during practice, and he was quick to give out punishments if things weren't to his liking.

These punishments were usually in the form of what he called "suicides." The late Herb Brooks, coach of the 1980 US gold medal hockey team, immortalized a form of suicides in the movie *Miracle* simply by saying, "AGAIN." Our suicides started at the end line in the gym. We would run to the free throw line and back, then to midcourt and back, then to the opposite free throw line and back, and finally to the far end and back. One was tough, five and someone was throwing up, and after ten someone usually passed out.

If we were outside, he would usually point to a tree somewhere in the distance and tell you to go and retrieve a leaf from it, and if it took too long, he would say, "No, that one is too small, go get a bigger one!" I never really understood why he would have a baseball team running so much; we used to complain to each other that we should all go out for the track team because we never saw them running as much as we were.

It wasn't until the season began that I realized what he had done with us. For one thing, no one ever questioned his decisions, and he always had our full attention, which helped keep us focused in the close games. Second, as a baseball team, we were never unprepared, outworked, or outhustled by the other team. We backed each other up on every play and learned to work as a unit both on offense and defense. No one ever came out of a game due to injury because no other team could hurt us as bad as our coach used to hurt us in practice. We were a baseball team with a football team's mentality.

Our work ethic started to pay off in the win column, and by midseason, after winning a close game with our cross-town rival, we were tied for first. It was at that point when Mr. Dick decided to step it up on the practice field, particularly with the suicides. I remember asking the coach that day if we did something wrong in the last game to deserve this punishment, and he shook his head and said, "No, but we always want to get better, 'cause if you're not getting better, then you are getting worse, and all the other teams out there that you just beat are working their tails off to get better for the next time they play us!"

We went on to win the city championship that year in dramatic fashion, and that was one of the highlights of my youth sports career. I will never forget those words, and to this day I still think about where I need to get better. "Good 'nuff" is the killer to constant improvement in business and in life. Once you have things going the way you want, the tendency is to just keep doing what you have always been doing and leave it alone.

I think about times in my professional and my personal life that I thought I could just maintain what I was doing and everything would be fine, but the harsh reality is that if you are not putting in the time and effort to constantly improve the things that matter the most to you, then ultimately those things will suffer.

Ben Franklin once said, "Success breeds complacency, and adversity breeds brilliance." The world is littered with talented individuals and organizations that settled for "good 'nuff," only to be recycled or replaced by something better or someone that worked harder. Every day, I think of one thing I can do to move a little closer to my goals, one little thing I can check off my list, one contact I can make in my professional life, one person I can call to tell how important he/she is to me, one little thing, one Quarter Turn, because in life if we aren't getting any better, then we are most definitely getting worse.

By the way, while Mr. Dick was our gym teacher and head coach, Mr. Ball was the industrial arts teacher and assistant coach. No joke, I couldn't make that up if I wanted to!

Ask yourself:

- Where in my life or business am I being complacent?
- In what areas am I settling for "good 'nuff"?
- What is or will be the impact of doing nothing?
- What am I willing to commit to this week to continue to get better?
- What Quarter Turn can I apply this week to move myself closer to my goal?

The Right Fight

Do you think it's possible for two people to look at the exact same thing and see completely different outcomes? Is it also possible for two people to look at the exact same thing, see completely different outcomes, and both be right? If you agree that both those situations are possible, then why do we always seem to get ourselves into "the right fight"? Both parties are right, yet neither is willing to concede that the other may be right as well.

If you have never been in the right fight, then I would say you have probably never been married or have a significant other in your life. Like many of you, I know I've found myself in this situation more than once. In fact, just recently my wife and I were having a discussion, and I was clearly right (in my own mind), but I began to realize that my being right was clearly hurting her feelings, and that certainly wasn't the outcome I was looking for. Still, it was hard for me to let go of my rightness in that situation. The challenge here is that for one party to be deemed "right," what does the other party have to be? You guessed it—WRONG! Let me ask you this: Do you enjoy being told that you are wrong? Didn't think so.

Are you the type of person that feels you always need to be right, or feels the need to prove to the rest of the world that you are right? Do you find yourself constantly on a mission to justify your "rightness" in many situations, defending your "right" positions, and creating conflict with your brilliant ability to be right in each and every scenario?

If you said yes to any of those, then I want to ask you a final value-based question: Have you ever been in a situation where you were absolutely 100 percent right about something and still didn't get the outcome you were looking for? How did that work for you?

There are many people out there that love to celebrate the fact that they are right, and judge themselves in most every situation on their ability to be right. The problem is they often find themselves with outcomes they don't intend and people around them feeling put down, let down, or shut down because they are tired of being made to feel wrong all the time.

Successful people and leaders have a unique ability to put aside their own competitive need and desire to be right in order to get the outcomes and results they are looking for. While that may sound very simple, it's actually one of the biggest obstacles to overcome in our journey toward success. Sadly, it's an obstacle that many talented, intelligent people never seem to overcome. A good friend of mine once told me, "You can be right, or you can have great relationships, but it's extremely difficult to have both."

Ask yourself:

- Is it more important for me to be right or to get the right outcome?
- Am I willing to sacrifice my need to be right, regardless of whether I actually am or not, to get the outcomes I am looking for?
- Can I concede that someone else may have a better solution that is different from mine but still gets the same (or an even better) result?

If you want to build a strong team at work, a better relationship at home, or create buy-in everywhere, then start by focusing on outcomes and letting go of the need to be right.

Stop Judging, Start Enjoying

Most, if not all, of us have relatives or people who are close to us—friends and acquaintances that just seem like they can't catch a break, or that they could be doing so much more with their lives. They have so much ability, but they just don't ever seem to use it or go where they need to go, and it's frustrating. Sometimes it's hard to watch.

I have a few relatives and friends that I care for deeply, and I would watch them meander around and never really do anything. In my view, they never really utilize even a tenth of what they could do. My disappointment got to the point where I almost didn't want to be around them because I would "anxietize" about it, and I would find myself trying to fix them or help them. I felt compelled to offer them solutions to problems that I felt they had, but it was to no avail, and it became a source of real tension for me.

I don't even know if they paid attention, but for me it was an issue until it dawned on me that I was the problem. They were happy and content and liked what they were doing, whatever it was. I was the one that had the problem. It was me. It wasn't them.

Understanding this was a bitter pill I had to swallow, because for all this time, I kept saying, "Boy, if they would only do this, or if they would only do that, or if they would just be this or just be that." It was ridiculous because it wasn't my life, and they were not asking me for my help.

One thing I've learned is that no matter how bad you want things for other people, no matter how bad you think they could do something, if they don't want to, if they're not interested in it, then it doesn't really matter. There is a tendency to frame the issue as though it is about you, but it's not.

One time, when I was on my way to visit one of these individuals, I told myself, "You know what? I'm not going to judge them. I'm not going to take all my baggage out on them and attempt to fix them or help them. I am just going to be with them and enjoy my time with them." And every time those old "fixing" thoughts popped into my head, I would say, "Hush up. Enjoy this person, because it's a person I immensely like being around." Once I did that, my visit was great. I let go of all that baggage and was able to just enjoy my time with that person.

It was a real eye opener and powerful Quarter Turn that said, "Make a choice. If you want to make this person part of your life, then stop judging and just start being with them. Find out what interests this person. And if your help is needed, I bet it will be asked for."

To return to my story, this person eventually started to find his path, and I had nothing to do with it. People do things at their own pace and in their own way. No matter how badly you want it for them or can see it through for them, they get to decide. It was a big lesson that I've taken with me for years. Today, my friends and all my family are people that I can enjoy in an honest and stress-free way.

Ask yourself:

- Who am I judging in my life, and how is that impacting the relationship?
- Why am I trying to fix and solve a problem for someone that isn't interested in my help? How's this working for me?
- Who am I going to stop judging and start enjoying?

Communication Breakdown

I speak with business leaders and human resource professionals all over the world, and based on the title of this section, I'm pretty sure you can guess what the number one reason is that I'm asked to come and work with an organization . . . that's right, communication. While communication is probably the most talked about word in business and relationships, I believe it is also the most misunderstood.

Like just about everything else in our lives, we fall into patterns and habits. Some of those habits are productive, and others are unproductive. The challenge we face is that our brains are essentially designed for sameness and duplication. Even when we are not really aware of it, our brain is creating patterns of thinking and habits to help us get through our days.

For example, think about the routine you have every day when you take a shower. I'm sure with a little thought you can probably write down exactly what you do, but it takes a little effort, right? But the minute you actually get into a shower and the water hits your face, you don't have to think for even one second about your routine, do you? Why? Because it's automatic.

Let's take it a step further. Think about what happens to you when your shower routine is interrupted. Maybe you reach for the soap and it is gone, or your shampoo is missing, or worst of all, you forgot to hang a towel close enough to reach for! Think how this completely throws you off and discombobulates you, even if only for a moment.

Many of our communication routines work exactly the same way. We may think about how we want to construct our interaction, plan it, or work through it, but the minute someone says or does something, like the water hitting our face, we just do what we've always done in the past. It's automatic! Worse, when someone does something we aren't prepared for, we get spooked like in the shower example, and we can become completely thrown off our game and discombobulated. This is usually when we say or do something that we later regret, often without even thinking about it. Productive or unproductive doesn't really matter in that moment; it's what we've always done.

This is how communication breaks down so easily and walls go up. Over time, a small misunderstanding or slight by the other party becomes a massive brick wall that becomes impossible to get over. Sometimes, in business and in our personal relationships, the breakdown becomes so great we bankrupt the organization or the relationship beyond repair.

The good news is our brains can be reprogrammed to help us create new and different outcomes, but we first have to decide what those outcomes are and whether or not we are committed enough to work toward those outcomes. Making the decision to build communication lines versus constantly breaking them down is always the first step.

Ask yourself:

- What communication barriers have developed in the relationships that mean the most to me?
- How am I contributing to the construction of this wall?
- What is the impact of this barrier?
- What outcome would I prefer in this relationship?
- What Quarter Turns am I willing to commit to this week to begin to break down those barriers and build the communication the way that I wanted?

The Biggest Objection is Usually Your Own

I once coached a young real estate agent who was really an amazing kid. He had only been in the business nine months and was already doing great. He could be on the phone and make calls all day to just about anyone. In sales, we call this "prospecting," and he was one of the best I had ever seen. In fact, he was so good he could set up an appointment with just about anyone he could get on the phone.

As a result of this, he started earning a significant income and was on his way to really becoming a great salesperson. The only thing that he felt was holding him back was that most of his home listings and sales were coming in the lower price ranges, so he had to sell twice as many homes to keep up with others. His goal then was to up his price range to the higher-value homes in his marketplace.

Since he was so good on the phone, he had no problem getting in front of these high-priced homeowners. His problem was that he was so young that he felt the homeowners never took him seriously and would never trust him to handle such a large transaction. The first question he would always get from these homeowners was "How old are you?" or "How long have you been selling real estate?" Once they asked this question, he would sulk and cower or get defensive and plead his case, but the damage was already done, and he never got any of those homes listed for sale.

As we worked through this challenge, what became very apparent was that the objection to his age and experience was really HIS objection! He really didn't think he was old enough or seasoned enough to handle these high-priced homes. He was extremely uncomfortable talking about them, and it showed in the conversations.

So I started to ask him different questions that he was more comfortable answering:

- *"Why are you the best person to handle the sale?"*
- *"What makes you different from all the other real estate agents?"*
- *"Why should we trust you?"*

All of which he could handle with no problem. Once we got back to age and experience, he crumbled . . . until we came up with the way to handle this specific objection in a way in that made him feel confident.

Question: *"How old are you?"*

Answer: *"Is it more important to you how old I am, or more important that you make the most money on the sale of your home?"* Objection overruled?

Question: *"How long have you been in the business?"*

Answer: *"Sometimes it feels like forever! Let me ask you, Mr. or Mrs. Seller, is it more important for you to have a real estate agent that uses old fashioned sales techniques, hasn't mastered modern technology, and basically thinks he can do things the way they have always been done, or would you prefer a young, hungry agent who works day and night, understands how to leverage technology, and was good enough at handling objections to get here in front of you today to list your home?"* BAM! Objection handled.

By coming up with the solutions to these two objections, this young man actually overcame them himself and was completely confident that he would be able to deal with this particular challenge when it came up.

Here is the most interesting part of the story. On his next two listing appointments, he used this objection handler, it worked perfectly for him, and he got the homes listed. But after those first two appointments, guess how many times he was asked how old he was or how much experience he had in the business? NEVER! It just never came up again.

Ask yourself:

- What objections do I have about my life, business, relationship, or money?
- How are they holding me back?
- What am I going to start telling myself to overcome these objections?

The Quarter Turn here is pretty obvious. The biggest obstacles we have in life are usually the ones we carry around with us. Once we get over them, amazingly, everyone else seems to as well.

Everyone is a Salesperson

I once coached a young director of a reality TV series. His goal was to venture away from bratty twentysomethings and their self-made drama and into his dream of directing feature films. I remember him boldly stating early on in the coaching process that he was not a "salesman," to which I gave a slight chuckle.

As we went through the process, what became clear to him was that selling is exactly what he did all day long. Working with young actors and reality stars to persuade and convince them to buy into his ideas and vision, working with edgy crewmembers to get the lighting and shots he wanted, dealing with insane producers to make them feel like they were part of the creative process, and convincing the network to give them extra time and money to create the show they were paying for. All of this sounds a lot like sales, doesn't it?

It was this realization that allowed him to go out and seek investors and "sell" them on his movie concept. He also persuaded young talent to work for much less than their going rates to be part of his amazing vision. Oh, and by the way, once he got his film shot, he had to go sell it again to distributors and film festivals, and then go out and sell it again to DVD and secondary markets. Yes, by the time it was over, there was no doubt he was a salesperson.

Guess what? You are too! Everyone is in sales, and no one on the planet is excluded. It all starts when we are kids, negotiating with our parents to buy us that souvenir, or persuading them to let us use the car, or to give us the later curfew. Then later on, as parents, we must learn to renegotiate the same things with our own kids. Have you ever discussed your grade with a teacher or challenged a question on the test? Guess what . . . you are selling. If you went to college, you probably built a long sales presentation to get accepted by the admissions office, and I bet you used one of your extracurricular activities, like student council, to "puff the goods," which just means making something sound much better than it really is.

Ever been to a job interview? You are doing your best to convince the person at the other end of the desk that you are the person that can solve all of their problems. Are you single? I bet you are selling someone out there online or in person to take an interest in you. Are you married? Well, then you already closed the deal! Let me ask you, how many photos did you sort through before you posted that perfect one on Facebook, LinkedIn, or whatever social network you are into? Why did you do that?

In the workplace, it's no different. No matter what your role is in the organization, you are constantly persuading and convincing your boss, your team, your peers, and even your customers and clients to buy into your thoughts, ideas, products, and solutions, aren't you?

Look, I'm sure some of you out there still believe that you are not in sales, and maybe you are right. Let me ask you this question, though. Would the quality of your business or your life improve just a bit if you mastered the art of convincing others, persuading others, negotiating with others, or influencing others?

If the answer is yes to any of these, then if you are not a salesperson, you'd better become one!

The New Normal

Back in the summer of 2001, our company was working with the organization that was responsible for bringing tourists to Las Vegas. They had developed a highly detailed plan, thought about it, put together action plans, and put a tremendous amount of time and effort into this plan. They voted on it, agreed on it, and finally got the budget approved. Everything was ready to go and then September 11 happened. What a tragic day that was for all of us that remember it.

Now, what do you think happened to that plan that had been so well thought out, prepared for, studied, and worked on? It got completely pitched out the window because it was no longer relevant. That was the first time in my professional life that I really understood just how radically organizations would need to adjust to the New Normal.

Do you remember how business stopped? Nobody knew what to do. Should I go to work? Should I not go to work? Should I cancel this? Should I postpone that? It took people about a week before anyone wanted to get on the phone again. And then from there, it took a couple months before people started realizing life goes on.

In the fall of 2008, in the midst of the biggest financial crisis since the Great Depression, I remember speaking to real estate agents, mortgage professionals, and financial planners and discussing the impact of this New Normal and how it has changed the face of their businesses. I remember the message was very consistent each time in that no matter how good it was before, because of the situation, things will never be the same. Never!

That doesn't mean they won't be good again. That doesn't mean things won't move forward. That doesn't mean that your business or your life won't flourish. But it will never be the same.

What I found then and still find today is that so many people and so many businesses start becoming nostalgic. "Well, gosh, I used to be able to do this, and I used to be able to do that, and man, it was so great then, and I remember when . . . "

That's okay, but know that circumstances may never be like that again, and the sooner you accept that, the easier it is for you to move on. While most everyone will agree that concept logically makes sense, it's much easier said than done.

You may be forced to completely reinvent the entire way you run your life or your business. While I agree that's usually not the case, because many of the basic underlying principals stay the same, I will also agree that the way you conduct yourself or the way you conduct business may need to change, and change rapidly.

The sooner you adjust, the quicker you'll be able to respond and flourish again. There are many companies and many people that never seem to make that adjustment, and then they find themselves going out of business or having to move on to something else because they either couldn't or wouldn't make the adjustment to this New Normal.

Think about the New Normal in your life. It may not be as dramatic as September 11, or the financial crisis of 2008 and 2009, but it has certainly had an impact on you. It could be the death of a loved one, a relationship ending, a son or daughter going off to school, changing a job, or moving. There are so many things that could have a big impact on your business and your life. How are you making adjustments to the New Normal?

Ask yourself:

- What systems or habits am I holding onto that are no longer working for me?
- What am I clinging to like an old blanket that's not getting me the outcomes I desire?
- Where am I missing new opportunities because of it?

Making adjustments to the New Normal, identifying what those habits and patterns are, and moving on can be very powerful. I didn't say it was easy, but it certainly has an impact.

Winning the Storage War

One of the best parts about what I get to do for a living is the amazing people that I get to meet along the way and how much I learn from them each and every day. I'm truly blessed to have so many contributors to my Quarter Turns, thanks to all of you!

I was training a group of leaders at a hotel and casino near Santa Fe, New Mexico. We were going through my customary "Tell Me Something Good" introductions, and someone shared a story about a friend he was helping clear out an old storage unit. He mentioned that his friend had been renting the unit for the past ten years or so, and he felt really good about assisting in this task. As the two began to sort through all of the miscellaneous items in the unit, one thing became perfectly clear—most of it was going directly into the trash bin. In fact, when all was said and done, the only contents that were saved were a few sentimental items that could be placed in two or three small boxes.

After the process, the man recounting this story did some quick math in his head and figured out that storing most of this worthless clutter for over ten years had cost his friend almost $18,000 in rental payments. That's right, $18,000! Both decided that that money could've gone toward a multitude of more valuable items during that same period.

As he shared this incredible story, I started to wonder just how much money I have wasted in my own life holding onto things of little or no value, and shuddered at the thought of the dollar amount. Then I started thinking about how much clutter I am currently holding onto everywhere else.

I thought about all the excess baggage I have carried around for so many years. All the guilt, pain, negative emotions, grudges, perceived slights, toxic relationships, and all of the other stuff that has long since passed the "use-by date." I started thinking about just how much this has cost me, and not just in dollars and cents, but in wasted energy and effort, stress, headache, physical pain, suffering, mental anguish, and just the vast amounts of time I burned through by holding onto all of this as though it carried some real value.

While there are some extremely valuable lessons that I have saved along the way that I will most certainly place in a small box, it became painfully clear to me that most of it was just trash that I have been holding onto and paying an excessively high rental payment for, which I have decided that I am no longer obligated to pay!

I made a pact with myself to begin the process of removing the excess clutter from my business and my life, so I could really focus on the things that matter to me the most: my family, my friends, the impact I can have on those I come into contact with, and most of all, this amazing journey called life. This is not a dress rehearsal, and we are not given a do-over, so why not lighten the load a bit?

Ask yourself:

- Where is the clutter in my life today?
- What's filling up the storage unit in my relationships or my business?
- What can I do this week to start clearing out trash?

Fear of Failure

Fear of failure is probably the biggest reason why so many of us choose to sell ourselves short and only put down goals that we are certain to accomplish. To use a golfing term, I call that "sandbagging." It causes us to aim right smack for the middle and never allows us to stretch or grow, and as a result we never really start down the road of accomplishing something amazing. Another year goes by and then we wonder, "Where did all the time go?" Sound familiar?

One of the biggest professional goals I have ever set for myself was to impact one million people, and I gave myself five years to do it. These types of goals or Big Rocks are usually referred to as BHAGS—big, hairy, audacious goals, and I think this one qualified.

I had no idea how I planned to get to this number or how I was going to go about it. I just knew that was what I wanted to accomplish. The number probably came from my days as a musician, because I always wanted to score a platinum record, which certifies one million record sales.

Unfortunately, I did not hit this goal. In fact, I missed it pretty big and came up about seven hundred thousand short. The thing is, I wasn't sad or upset in the least. Sure, I was a bit disappointed, but as I reflected on those five years, I realized all of the things I've learned and accomplished in the pursuit of this big, hairy, audacious goal.

When I began pursuing this goal, the Quarter Turns brand didn't exist, so I'd brought a new business into the world, and guess what? It's still here! I've also built a website, and I am in the process of building new ones constantly.

During that same period, I developed the Virtual Coach, which has allowed me to coach hundreds of people at one time on over five continents.

I'm no longer in the category of what I call "digitally intimidated," as I have embraced all this amazing technology. (Thank you, Steve Jobs!)

In the pursuit of this goal, I also created several new keynote presentations that allowed me to enter new markets and new companies and develop a reputation as a speaker that can kick off or end a conference with a supercharged burst of energy.

By the way, this book you are now reading is a direct result of that particular goal.

I accomplished all of this and so much more as a result of creating this really big goal. You see, it's not the goal that actually makes the difference; it's the person that you become as a result of putting it out there that uncovers all the incredible Quarter

Turns in life and in business. As for impacting a million people, don't worry, I will get there. Maybe by the time you read this I will have surpassed that goal. Hopefully I get to count you as one more!

As you reflect on this topic, create your goals for the next year. Go back to the chapter in the book where you created your goals, and be sure to include at least one BHAG. See where it takes you. I've heard it said that we tend to overestimate what we can accomplish in one year and underestimate what we can accomplish in five years. Where do you want to be in five years?

With respect to the memory of the late Zig Ziglar, here are some things to think about and some of his best quotes:

- *"Remember that failure is an event, not a person."*
- *"You will get all you want in life if you help enough other people get what they want."*
- *"There has never been a statue erected to honor a critic."*
- *"Expect the best. Prepare for the worst. Capitalize on what comes."*
- *"If you go looking for a friend, you're going to find they're scarce. If you go out to be a friend, you'll find them everywhere."*
- *"Your attitude, not your aptitude, will determine your altitude."*
- *"If you can dream it, you can achieve it."*

Now that we've identified a few of the many obstacles that can crowd our path to success, I'm sure you would agree that fear of failure can certainly be one of the most challenging. Once you overcome that fear, it is easier to begin to develop a strategy toward your success.

Section 4

Strategy

Congratulations, you have done some amazing work so far. You have created awareness, developed some clarity, and identified a few of your obstacles. You have laid a solid foundation for obtaining your goals. Now it's time to start working on a strategy to get you exactly what you want. You've done the internal work, now it's time to start executing your plan in the external world. This is where it gets exciting!

What is a strategy? Simple; it's a clearly defined plan with action items, time lines, details, and solutions to problems already clarified, and finally, the will to get it done!

As we start working on strategy and moving toward your goals, you will notice the sense of accomplishment in achieving the small steps that occur along the way. You may also uncover some paths to other goals that have eluded you in the past. This is an added bonus that you gain, and it is all part of the process. Now is the time to stop talking and start walking, stop complaining and start sweating! If you are ready to keep moving forward, then soon you will get to cross the goal line, spike the ball, and do your own touchdown dance. So what are you waiting for? This Quarter Turn is all about getting strategic.

No One Is as Committed to Your Success as You

One of the many valuable lessons I've learned in my career is that no matter what anybody tells you, no one, and I mean NO ONE, can possibly be as committed to your success as you are. This is a lesson I had to learn the hard way during my days as a touring musician.

Being on the road with my band in my early twenties was my first venture out into the real world. What I didn't know back then was that almost everyone that we came into contact with that claimed they could help us become successful usually had an ulterior motive. Some secretly wanted to be a musician or associate with the entertainment industry is some way. Others had been part of a successful group early in their careers but were cut out when the fame and fortune started to kick in. They were looking to find the "next big thing" that they could attach their anchor to, sign them up to some sort of agreement that screwed the band, and give themselves what they deserved with the first group that screwed them. It's all a big cycle—as I soon learned.

Consequently, everyone we came into contact with believed they were our ticket to the big time. "If you just listen to me, kid, I'll take you to the top. Just sign this and all your dreams will come true!" Now I wasn't that naive, and my band and I knew that if it sounded too good to be true, it usually was, so we avoided signing any long-term contract that would give all of our rights away to someone else. We did, however, put our trust and faith into several individuals that sounded legit and seemed to have the proof to go along with it.

Our mistake was that we worked so hard to get noticed and when everything was heading in the right direction, we would allow someone else to take the reins, which would put a halt to our momentum. Months later we would realize this person wasn't doing anything he said he would do, and we would have to start all over again.

We were young and had tons of energy, so it just seemed like this was the price we had to pay for success. We assumed, like in the movies, that someone would just come along and discover us and all our brilliance and that would be that. Unfortunately for me, this was a lesson I seemed to have to keep learning over and over again, sometimes with the same person over and over again, before I realized that no one was going to work as hard as I to get what I wanted.

The other problem this created was it allowed me to blame others for the reason I wasn't successful or obtaining my goals, and there is nothing productive about that.

The reality is, by the time I finally internalized this huge Quarter Turn, my window as a musician seemed to have passed, and it was time to move on, but the lesson has proven valuable in my life. I would no longer entrust any one person or entity with my personal success. Today, I determine my success. Don't get me wrong, I am willing to accept help, advice, support, and anything else offered to me in the pursuit of my goals. I just have no expectation that someone is going to do it for me.

Ask yourself:

- Where in my life am I waiting around for someone else to dictate the terms of my success?
- Who am I blaming as the reason I haven't moved forward or grown?
- What impact has this mentality had on me and those around me?
- What Quarter Turns am I willing to commit to this week to take control of my outcomes?

Whom Do You Trust?

I've often said that being a musician prepared me for a career in sales because I learned to handle rejection extremely well. People ask me all the time about lessons that I learned during the years I spent touring the country, writing songs, and recording them, and I can tell you for a fact that I would not have the success I have today without my music experience.

One powerful lesson was having someone else that I trusted enough to share my creative vision and understood what it would take to get where I wanted to go. My guitarist and song-writing partner Donnie was that partner, and I learned to trust him implicitly.

Together we wrote hundreds of songs and recorded many of them, but one of the rules we had was brutal honesty. If the idea stunk, then it was the obligation of the other party to say so: no candy coating, just the truth. It was the other's responsibility to never allow that honesty to cause hurt feelings or internal problems.

If you felt strongly enough about the idea, you were given the opportunity to make an argument, and if it was compelling enough, then we worked through it, but ultimately we both had to come to an agreement that the idea was good enough before we would present it to the others in the band.

That rule served us well because it allowed us to sort through a lot of ideas quickly—no egos, no fights—and the final product was always much better as a result.

In my coaching practice, I find that so many leaders do not have that person in their organization that is willing to be brutally honest with them, and the business suffers as a result. Before I begin to work with a new coaching client, I have them answer this important question: "Do you want me to tell you what you want to hear or what you NEED to hear?" Of course they always want me to tell them what they need to hear, to which I respond, "Be careful what you wish for!"

Ask yourself:

- Whom do I trust in my business?
- Are people able to be brutally honest with me?
- Do people tell me what I want to hear or what I need to hear?
- How am I responding when people are honest with me?
- Is my ego getting in the way?

If you do not have that person in your business and in your life, then I suggest you find them!

The Best Leaders Are Usually the Best Listeners

Here's something that should not come as a shock to you: I've been fortunate enough in my career to work with some amazing leaders and some really amazing people. One of the common denominators for all of them was that they seem to fall into the best listener category most of the time. I'm not going to kid you, I've seen and worked with successful leaders that are poor listeners as well, but the difference is that they tend to burn through people and relationships very quickly and often create toxic cultures and relationships. Is that what you are looking for?

When you are not paying close attention, it's easy to miss the real message. How often do people say something that they actually don't really mean or that means something else? There are studies that suggest when you're communicating with somebody, less than 50 percent of your message is conveyed by the words you are using. That means the rest of your message is conveyed nonverbally. It's conveyed through your body language, through your tone, through your actions, through what you're doing. Not just the words you're using.

I'll prove it. How many times have you attempted to solve a really tense or complicated issue via e-mail? How did that work for you? No matter how much we explain or overexplain in an e-mail, the words are often misinterpreted, or your receiver latches onto a word or sentence that wasn't even part of your intended message.

I can even give you the reason: it's because we are human beings! You see, our brains will attach that last real human interaction we have had with the other person to whatever words are being said in the e-mail. If the interaction wasn't very good, then we attach that negative emotion to the e-mail. It's also because when we write our e-mails, we are usually saying the words in our head and in doing so, we are attaching meaning, value, sarcasm, humor, and emphasis on certain words and phrases. Well, guess what the receiver of your message is doing? The exact same thing. Only their meanings, values, sarcasm, humor, and emphasis may not match up to yours.

If you think about listening in general, we've all become professionals at not listening and not paying attention. We're doing other things on our computers or smartphones or answering our text messages while there's a person right in front of us. All of our digital toys, designed to keep us connected, are actually creating barriers and making it harder to communicate.

I was out at a social event, and there was a group of people that got together for dinner. Everyone was looking down at smartphones, banging away a message to someone else. No one was bothering to communicate with the people that they decided to take time out of their busy lives to be with. It's like saying, "You're not as important as the person who's not here." Isn't that interesting? Or crazy?

Ask yourself:

- What listening habits have I gotten into? Will they put me in the best or worst listener category?
- In which situations in my life is it the hardest for me to actually pay attention? Why?
- What has been the impact of my failure to listen to those around me?
- What am I going to do about it?

Time to put down that smartphone, turn away from that computer screen, and really listen to the person you are talking to face-to-face.

Where Are Your Blind Spots?

As I have already stated, one of the biggest goals I've ever committed to is impacting the lives of over one million people and essentially going platinum. This book is a direct result of that commitment. Probably the most eye-opening Quarter Turn that I have identified during this ambitious pursuit is that in order for me to do it, I'm going to need a lot of help.

I used to describe myself as digitally intimidated, but the only way I was going to be able to impact such a large volume of people in the quickest amount of time would be through extensive use of the Internet. The problem was that I'm not a web expert and certainly not a marketing genius, so those were two areas in which I would require some help and support.

This realization caused me to hire an online marketing and web-business coach to help build my website and integrate everything into one spot. I can tell you that giving up control of something that I was very passionate about was a big step for me, and it wasn't an easy conclusion to get to. Now that I am committed to the process of using and trusting talented individuals to do what they do best, it seems so obvious, especially since I've coached many others to do just that. The one thing I know for certain is that this decision has helped me accomplish goals that are way outside of my skill set.

I've also utilized the help of organizational and editorial people that I know and trust to bring this book to you. Without their help, there is no way you would be reading this today. Again, these amazing people bring skills and knowledge to the table that I simply do not possess. Recognizing this and then taking action has helped me fill in the blind spots in my own life and career.

High achievers and high performers consistently surround themselves with people that fill in the gaps or have strengths where they have a weakness or blind spot. All great relationships seem to have a yin-and-yang quality about them that allow each person to excel at a higher level than they ever could on their own. Successful people clearly understand that for them and their organizations to be successful, they cannot do it alone.

Ask yourself:

- Where are my blind spots?
- Where am I not utilizing people or resources that complement my own skills?
- Where am I unable to ask for help?

Developing and embracing this Quarter Turn can greatly accelerate your progress in accomplishing the outcomes you desire.

Intention versus Impact

My belief is that human beings are basically living, breathing double standards based on a simple concept: intention versus impact.

I assume that most people have good intentions. The vast majority of people in this world, in my experience, really do not intend to be malicious. Maybe some people do, but for the most part people tend to make decisions and operate based on their own good intentions.

Think about this for a minute: if we act or make a decision based on our own good intentions, and that decision impacts someone else in a negative way, do we judge ourselves by our intentions or our impact?

Some suggest they judge themselves purely based on their impact; I would submit that is a load of you-know-what, because the first thing out of our mouths when we negatively impact others is, "Oh, I'm sorry, that's not what I meant to happen," or "That wasn't my intention." We may even feel bad, but since we know our intentions were good we tend to judge ourselves on those criteria alone.

Here is where the double standard, and its subsequent paradox, exists: when others make decisions based on their own good intentions and that decision has a negative impact on us, in that moment do we judge them based on their good intentions or their impact on us? I think you get the picture. The truth is that even when we understand the intentions, we still have a hard time letting go of the impact those actions had on us.

Does that make any sense? Should you judge yourself based on your good intentions alone? Are you giving other people the benefit of the doubt or showing interest in finding out what that person's intentions were by asking questions, listening to the answers, and allowing the real intent to come out? Or are you so busy being pissed off about the impact it had on you that you don't even bother asking? Are you simply reacting to the impact? If so, how's that working for you?

More importantly, are you making decisions in your life and in your workplace based on the impact you want, or are you too busy congratulating yourself about your good intentions?

If you're still pondering this, allow me to remove the suspense: successful individuals and organizations are only thinking about impact!

Throw your good intentions right out the window. I will assume you have good intentions (if you genuinely do not have good intentions, then I have a completely different book for you). You can no longer lead or live your life based on your good intentions, because impact is the only thing that counts and, quite frankly, the only thing those around you will ever remember.

Ask yourself:

- What is the impact of my decisions on my business, my friends, my family, me?
- How is that impact matching up with my good intentions?
- What Quarter Turns can I apply to be an impact player in all facets of my life?

Hit the Pause Button

Doesn't it feel like life is moving excessively fast these days? So much is coming at us all at once that it feels like information overload. In a conversation with one of my clients, we likened the pace of the modern workplace to the feeling of having a 95 mph fastball from a major league pitcher being thrown right at your head every day. The real challenge is that the pitches are often coming from multiple directions and at the same time, so we don't even know where and when to duck anymore!

I read a study that suggests 80 percent of ALL illness can be traced back to some form of stress and that 60 percent more people feel excessive amounts of stress in their lives than they did back in 1990. I'm sure none of this comes as a surprise to you since you are probably feeling stress to read this quickly and get back to the fray.

As my mind was working through this very real and relevant topic, something became clear to me. We put so much unhealthy pressure on ourselves and those around us to complete EVERYTHING that has been thrown at us, and it's this attempt to do it all at once that creates the bulk of the stress in our lives.

I understand that everyone has goals and tasks that we wish to accomplish—in fact, I coach my clients to have specific goals. Yet every day, more and more piles up while the old tasks still linger, and the new task is now taking the focus. We start to dread getting up the next day because we already know about the new task that's on the books, and we haven't even taken into account the surprise tasks that we don't even know about but are sure to come our way soon! Wow, sound familiar? No wonder we are so tired and stressed these days. I get exhausted just writing about it!

The reality check for me is that I have been heaping all this stress to get things completed over to my family and my personal life. Pushing everyone to do everything that we planned only to add more the next day, creating additional stress and the feeling that I'm losing track of my goals and what is really important. I found myself looking for small gaps of time in the family schedule just to squeeze something else in, to do even more. This insanity simply has to stop, because it is not working for me. How about you?

I have a new Quarter Turn that is simply this: hit the pause button. When I sense that my work or personal schedule is getting way out of control, I'm simply going to stop that cycle. It's not that I'm going to toss all of my goals and plans out the window; it's just that some things that come up take precedent and need to be addressed right then and there.

That also doesn't mean that the old plan is bad or not as important. I'm just not going to cram all that into the day simply because it was a goal of mine and had a set date that I wanted it completed by. For those less pressing tasks, I'm just going to hit the pause button and resume the task when time makes it appropriate to do so, that's it.

Ask yourself:

- Where do I need to hit the pause button in my business or in my life?
- Where am I cramming too much into the schedule?
- What tasks can I lay off of for a while to focus on the 95 mph fastballs I will need to deal with today?
- What will be the net result if I choose to keep overloading my schedule? Is that the outcome I am looking for?

Making these tiny Quarter Turns and adjustments to your schedule can have a huge impact on the quality of your work and your life.

Pick Your Battle

I went back to school to finish up the college degree that I promised both my parents I would obtain if the "music thing" didn't pan out the way I had hoped.

During those years in school, I took a job as an after-school childcare counselor. Excluding my current job, this was probably the greatest job I ever had, since I was just a big kid myself. They actually paid me every day to go to the gym, do art projects, and play on the playground . . . with kids! How great is that?

The problem was it didn't pay very well. I needed to earn some extra money, so I took a second job near the university at another elementary school as a lunchroom coordinator. I was, as they say, "the mean old lunch lady." Just about everyone I know has a memory of the mean old lunch lady, except I was different: I was the cool young lunch guy.

In this job, I learned how to manage both small and large groups of kids, and I also learned how to effectively discipline kids. This skill has really helped me raise my own kids, because I learned that kids really like boundaries and structure, even when it seems like they are so upset and rebellious regarding rules. They will act like it is the end of the world, but deep down they respect you and you have a stronger relationship with them because you took the time to help them correct their behavior. Obviously, that was a huge Quarter Turn for me, but we will leave that for another time.

Knowing I had an impact on some pretty great kids would have been enough to make the experience worthwhile (that and dodgeball in the gym), but my time as the lunchroom coordinator put me into contact with another amazing leader—Mrs. Williams, the school principal.

Next to my mother, Mrs. Williams was by far the best principal I had ever seen. I have a few school districts as clients today, and I watch school administrators struggle to find just the right balance in leadership, so I've come to appreciate her even more. Obviously, the kids liked her, but she had the full support of the teachers, maintained full support from the parents, all the while working seamlessly with the administration. Anyone in the public school system would know that is no small accomplishment. In the business world, we would say she manages up, down, and sideways extremely well—again, a rare feat.

I watched her perform her many challenging roles on a daily basis for almost two years in some trying circumstances. It was there that I first learned about leadership in the trenches. One day, in particular, it seemed like the perfect storm. Budget cuts were looming, kids were getting hurt on the playground, angry parents from the parent-teacher organization were banging on the door, and a teacher that had waited a month to discuss a minor grievance was clamoring for face time.

In those five minutes, I watched her zig and zag and address every issue. She dismissed some, delegated others, and she confronted the remaining issue head on, doing whatever it took to make the situation workable.

When the commotion finally died down, I went to her, utterly blown away by her ability to handle multiple fires at once, and I asked her how she managed herself in situations when everything comes at the same time. I'll never forget her response. She said, "You know, Tim, sometimes I just have to ask myself: Which hill am I willing to die on today?"

I just love the simplicity of that statement: focus on what you can, focus on what is important to achieve your goal in the moment, and let go of all the other things until another day. As I watch executives and leaders that I work with today, I find many of the successful ones have learned this strategy and apply it regularly. Some things will just have to wait till tomorrow. Thanks, Mrs. Williams, for teaching me this early in my career.

Each day, when you are confronted with your work, kids, health, money, relationships—pick the hill you plan to die on, and make sure it's the right one.

Ask yourself:

- What single focus am I going to concentrate on today?

- Which important tasks may have to wait until another time?
- How do I prioritize what truly needs my energy and focus, and what can I delegate to others?
- What small Quarter Turns am I going to take toward my most important goals today?

Feedback Loop

Have you ever been given feedback on your behavior or maybe something you have done that was extremely difficult to hear? How did you react to it? If you are a human being, then I would guess you probably didn't react to it the way you wish you would have now that you have had a chance to look back on it. I would also venture to say that while that feedback wasn't very pleasant for you to hear, you probably gained a lot of value from it and have become a better person for having received it.

The fact of the matter is that someone gave you an incredible gift with that feedback, and at some point before it's all said and done, you may want to seek that person out and say thank you. Just imagine how hard it was for that individual to drum up the courage to say what they said to you. What would your life be like today if they had not shared that feedback with you? Would you be better off today having never received it?

Giving and receiving feedback can be a very difficult and gut-wrenching experience, but it's the only way we can get any better.

Feedback, both positive and constructive, is an amazing gift. When we are given a gift, it's always appropriate to say thank you. Making this one Quarter Turn allows you to constantly make improvements in your business and your life. Encouraging others to give you this feedback ensures that you will continue to receive this gift for the rest of your life.

Ask yourself:

- Who has given me valuable feedback that I have either dismissed or devalued?
- What caused that person to give that feedback?

- How did I react when they gave it to me?
- How would I react today if given it again?
- Who am I depriving of feedback in my life and in my business?
- Why aren't I willing to give this person the gift of my feedback?
- How do I plan to consistently give and receive feedback in the coming weeks and months?

Just Smile and Move On

It probably will not surprise you that the number one fear most people have is public speaking. What surprises me is that the number two fear of most people is death by fire! Taken literally, that means, if given a choice, there are more people that would rather be burned alive than speak in front of an audience.

This interesting fact is one of the reasons why I designed a Public Presentation Bootcamp for companies that I work with. That seminar is filled with many of the lessons I've learned in my twenty-seven plus years of performing on stages with my various bands and doing what I do now in speaking at conferences and seminars all around the world.

One of my favorite little tips I learned came from my former bass player who also happens to be named Tim. Tim was an amazing musician who actually performed in symphony orchestras, but much to the disappointment of the University of Michigan Music Department, he walked away from a music scholarship to pursue his rock and roll dream along with my bandmates and I.

It probably will come as no surprise that as a young lead singer in a fairly successful band, I was a pretty cocky little kid. In music we call it "Lead Singer-itis." As a result of this ailment, I had developed a bad habit of looking directly at any member of the band that missed a part during a song and showing my disapproval of the mistake with a stern look or scowl. Much like a referee in a football game, I would basically throw a yellow flag anytime something happened that I didn't like, thus alerting the entire world that someone had screwed up.

One day at rehearsal, Tim, who was much more seasoned at actually playing to live audiences, pulled me aside and asked me to do him a favor. "Hey, Tim," he said, "we are all up there on stage doing our best to put on an amazing show for the audience, but we are all going to make mistakes at times. The thing is, when I miss a part, I always know it, but when you give me a nasty look like that, you let EVERYONE else know it, and that makes me feel self-conscious, and I can't perform very well. What I like to do when I make a mistake is just smile and move on. Usually no one in the audience really knows what I'm supposed to be playing anyway, so they never realize I actually made a mistake! Do you think you could do that for me?"

There were so many lessons I learned from that piece of feedback. First, it got my ego in check right away, because rather than calling me an outright jerk, he basically said, "When you do this, it makes me feel this way." What a great way to have a potentially difficult conversation with someone. Second, I learned one of the best ways to overcome a fear most people have about speaking in front of an audience, which is what to do when they make a mistake. I have made thousands of mistakes in front of thousands of people and will continue to do so, but each and every time I just smile and move on. Guess what? Most people never know the difference.

Ask yourself:

- How am I reacting when those around me make mistakes? When I make a mistake?
- What is the impact on their performance? How about my own performance?
- Where in my life do I need to give someone feedback about their bad behavior?
- When am I going to have that conversation that starts with "When you do this, it makes me feel this way"?

Remember, mistakes happen and sometimes it's best to smile and move on.

Make the Tough Calls First

Many years ago, at a sales conference where I was invited to speak, one of the other guest speakers told the audience that the first thing he did in the morning was to make the hardest phone calls first—the really tough ones that he knew were going to cause him a lot of grief, headache, and stress. As he was explaining his process, I was thinking that it made a lot of sense to me, because I know myself, and I know how I am about those types of calls. One of my favorite speakers and authors, Brian Tracy, actually wrote a book about this same topic called *Eat That Frog!*

What happens when we don't make those tough phone calls first? We sit there all day, we stew over it, we anxietize over it, we stress about it, and we build it up until it becomes this massive event. And then, when we finally get around to making the call, it's usually—at least in my experience—never as bad as we built it up to be. Yet it cost me a lot in anxiety and increased my stress levels. It's an expensive phone call that would have been far less costly had I made it earlier.

I've taken that a step further to include dealing with virtually all situations in my life that aren't really that comfortable and not that much fun. I began to address them right away, and in some cases, as soon as they showed up on my "radar screen." I know it's something that's going to cause me some amount of stress, but it will be much less stressful if I just take care of it right then and there rather than if I put it off.

The Quarter Turn is to deal with it now! Don't wait. If you do, over time things will just build up inside, and it becomes a huge event that you attach so much to. And when you finally get around to it, it's never what you expected. It's usually not nearly as bad, and many times it's actually a good thing. Taking that simple idea and applying it in my life has reduced my stress level tremendously.

I once read a study that suggested we create up to 50 percent of the stress in our lives all by ourselves . . . 50 percent! Would it have an impact on your life to reduce your stress level by 50 percent? That's what I thought. Besides, when you make those tough calls first, it seems to make everything else that day so easy.

On a slightly different but related topic, there was this gentleman that I came to know who was just an amazing person and excellent speaker. His first name is Bob. When Bob would get a really nasty voicemail, he would not even listen to it. He would just delete it and wait about an hour or two to call the person back. Bob would then say, "Hey, I saw that you left a message. Unfortunately it got deleted. It was all garbled, I couldn't understand it. So what did you have to say there? What did you need?" He said that in almost every instance, the people were usually relieved that he never heard that voicemail. They would start telling him a more sanitized version of their concerns in a way so that Bob could better understand the problem they needed solved without having to deal with the drama.

Bob realized it didn't matter how upset they were, because he couldn't do anything about it until he talked to them. So he would just delete it. Get rid of it. And follow up with no knowledge of the original complaint.

I've started doing the same thing with e-mails. I say, "You know what? I'm not going to read this anymore. I'm just going to delete it because I'll get angry and upset and stressed. I'll only see what I want to see, so instead I will call the person and say I was confused by the e-mail so I thought I'd call to clarify, or say we're having IT issues today." (Sorry, IT people.) "We lost a bunch of old e-mails, and yours was one of them. What's going on?" Again, people are usually a lot more cordial at that time.

So make the tough calls first and don't take those nasty messages personally. Remember, people don't do things to you, they do things for themselves. Just smile and move on!

Just Say Thank You!

Are you the type of person that has a hard time saying thank you when someone tells you that you did a good job? Do you get uncomfortable when anyone decides to give you a compliment? Surprisingly, you are not alone. I've coached countless numbers of extremely successful people who have trouble hearing anything good about themselves. They immediately discount the compliment with "Ah, shucks" or "That was nothing" or "I could've done better" or "Just doing my job."

Where does that come from? I'm not a psychotherapist and would never pretend to be one, but my belief is that somewhere along the line we confused being good at something or recognizing a job well done with bragging or boasting. Everyone knows someone in his or her life that always seemed to take unearned credit or always wanted to be the center of attention and, well, who likes that?

The problem is we tend to go to the extreme opposite and never allow ourselves or anybody else to appreciate what we are bringing to the table. We never stop to say good job to ourselves or hear it from others. We never get to cross the goal line, spike the ball, and do our touchdown dance. What is the payoff for that type of behavior? Stress, tension, and an underlying sense that no matter what we do, it's not going to be good enough. Sound familiar to anyone?

We keep moving the line of perceived success until it becomes some mythical, unattainable entity never to be achieved, and certainly never celebrated. Somehow we've confused the need to get better and improve, which is a good thing, with never being good enough in the moment, which is painful and dysfunctional. Think of the long-term impact on us, on those that are close to us, on those that work with us or for us?

What message are we sending to our kids, our significant others, and our coworkers? Remember those around you and close to you will do what you do, not what you say. Is that really the message you want to convey? Are those the lessons you want to pass along to your teams and your families? Your only job, when someone decides to go out of their way to give you a compliment or tell you great job, from this day forward is to say these two words . . . THANK YOU!

It's the least you can do for that person. The next step would be for you to take ten seconds and give yourself a silent pat on the back. After all, isn't that the least you can do for yourself?

Ask yourself:

- Where am I discounting all the amazing gifts and talents that I bring to the table?
- How do I respond when people go out of their way to tell me job well done?
- What message am I conveying to those around me? Is that the message I want to send?

These Are Not the Droids You Are Looking For

It's no secret that I really believe everything begins with having the right attitude and energy, but creating the outcomes you are looking for is about a lot more than just having a positive attitude. I know many people who tell me, "I always have a positive attitude, but things don't always work out." Well, it's one thing to say it to yourself, it is another thing to actually believe it, and that is the big separator in success versus failure. The difference maker is the belief, not just constant positive affirmations. Ultimately, you really have to believe it.

I like to use that story from the original *Star Wars* movie—yes, I am a *Star Wars* geek. Remember when Obi-Wan and Luke are traveling into the city, and Luke was so worried about being discovered by the Storm Troopers? "Oh no, they are going to find us out." And Obi-Wan says, "Don't worry about it, we'll be fine." He just knew that he was going to get past the guards. Remember when he says, "These are not the droids you are looking for. We can pass, let us go through," and they just passed right through the gate?

I reflect on this story with a lot of my coaching clients. "These are not the droids you are looking for." You really get to believe in your mind that what you want, you are going to get. Really believe it! Right down to your core, there can be no doubt that you will actually get what you want. Once that happens, then everything else kind of falls into line. You can call that spiritual, you can recite the book *The Secret*, whatever works for you, but your brain is programmed to identify and confirm things in the outside world that support what you believe on the inside.

I will give you an example of a time that this has worked out for me, and it was with basketball tickets, of all things. I have been to hundreds and hundreds of games in my lifetime, growing up with my father and now going to games with my two sons. I have always had tickets, and I had never in my life lost a ticket. My dad always said, "You got your ticket?" and I would say, "Yeah, Dad, I got my ticket."

One winter day I was with some friends, and we were going to the Michigan-Michigan State college basketball game. It was the biggest game of the year. Michigan State is always a contender, and Michigan was in a rebuilding year, looking to knock them off. This was one of the few sold out games of the year at Crisler Center in Ann Arbor. My friend, John, had four tickets and they were great seats right at center court, about as good as you can get unless you are actually playing in the game.

We were out at a restaurant before the game, talking about the players, having some fun, and John gave out the tickets and said, "Okay, now don't lose your ticket," just like my dad used to do. Everyone was laughing, and I said in my best little-kid voice, "Okay, thanks, Dad," in a very joking manner.

We got to the game and I reached into my back pocket, and sure enough, it was gone. I started reaching around, panicking, reaching around, oh no! Sure enough, I had lost my first ticket ever! Of all the games to lose it, of all the times to lose it—we were ten minutes from tip off. We had timed it perfectly, and here I was with no ticket. My big joke with my dad, and well, finally it happened to me.

We decided to put our little theory to the test. John and I both knew how strong the power of intention can be, and we said, "You know, we are just going to go up, and we are going to get in—period!" We looked at each other and kind of laughed because there was not a doubt in our minds that we were going to get into this game. There was just no doubt. There were three of us with tickets and me without, but there was no doubt we were all going to walk through the door. Now if there had been any doubt, I can guarantee you I would not have been watching a game that night.

I know that some of you have said, "Well, I have done that before, and it didn't work out." I would challenge you that somewhere in the back of your mind was a voice telling you there was no way you were getting through this door. "There is no way this is going to happen. What are you thinking?" Even though you were telling yourself in a positive affirmation, "I know I can, I know I can, I know I can," you didn't believe it. Well, we believed it. John believed it. I believed it.

As we walked up, we wanted to select the right person, with the right energy. One guy looked angry and mean. You don't want to talk to that guy. He has the wrong energy. Another guy had a funky look on his face, so he was out too. Then we saw this pleasant looking gentleman, and he had the right energy. We walked right up to him, and we told him our story. He first looked at us and said, "You've got be joking, right? You want to get in here without a ticket? This is the only sold-out game of the year." We said, "You know, this is really okay. We've got it. We know. It's covered. These aren't the droids you're looking for," and sure enough, he looks right at us and says, "OK, just don't tell anybody."

That is a true story. I did not make that up. I knew what the result was going to be before it happened. If you can learn this at a young age, and practice this idea of focusing on the desired outcome, it's extremely powerful. It's creating a belief that the end result is going to be exactly the way you want it to be. A real belief that "things always work out for me."

Today, I travel all over the world, and I can tell you that I've gotten on planes, checked into rooms, rented cars, when at first it seemed there was no possible way I could. Even the person that gives me what I've asked for can't believe it at the time they hand over the ticket or reservation. "These aren't the droids you're looking for. It's OK. I can pass through."

There is a big difference between positive affirmations and the belief that things will go the way you want them to—never forget that. The best part of the story is that Michigan actually won that game!

Give Yourself a Do-Over

Do you remember when you were a kid playing a game of kickball and there would be that play that was just too close to call? Then usually, after both sides had argued the point without resolution, what did you used to do? That's right, you said, "Do-over!"

Over the years I've been privileged to work with some amazing individuals, successful business owners, leaders of large organizations, solo entrepreneurs, realtors, and rockstars, each with their own unique styles and recipes for success. There is a common theme that I have noticed with all of them, though, and it's that they have all made many mistakes and failed numerous times throughout their careers. The big difference with these high achievers is that rather than wallow in the muck, beat themselves up, blame the unfair world, or waste precious time and energy being unproductive, they tend to look at those situations as learning opportunities.

Though I've heard it told in many different ways, successful individuals will look at every situation that doesn't work out for them, define exactly what happened, decide what they wanted the outcome to be, then challenge themselves to decide what they will do differently when presented with a similar situation.

Finally, and probably most importantly, they will actually APPLY the lesson when the situation arises. I realize this all sounds really fancy, but basically they give themselves a mental do-over. Most will do this without even realizing it, because it's just become so ingrained as a habit. You can make this a habit as well, but it only comes naturally with a lot of practice.

Think about a situation over the past few weeks where you didn't get the result you were looking for, maybe in your business, with a coworker, your boss, spouse, kid, even a friend or extended family member. Ask yourself what happened. Then decide what outcome you would have liked. Practice exactly what you will do and say if confronted with the same situation again. Then simply apply what you learned. Simple, right? Just like when you were a kid. Call a do-over.

Ask yourself:

- What happened?
- How did I respond when it happened?
- What outcome did I get as a result?
- What outcome would I have preferred?
- How will I respond in the future to get my desired outcome?
- What is the lesson I am supposed to learn from this?
- How will I apply this in the future?

Give yourself as many do-overs as necessary until the Quarter Turn becomes a habit.

Sometimes Just Being There Is Enough

I remember when I was in high school, one of my best friend's grandmothers passed away. They were very close, and he was taking it really hard. There was a lot of crying and sadness, as is to be expected. Being that this was my best friend, I really wanted to help him get through it, but to be honest with you, I was only sixteen and did not have a clue what I could do. Every time I said something it came out goofy, but I kept thinking I could say something that would ultimately let him know that I cared and would do anything that I could to help get him through this terrible event.

Finally, I realized my efforts were in vain, and I just sort of quit doing or saying anything. All I could think to do was just be there and sit quietly and let him grieve. I did this for two days, during the showing and at the service, and finally at the cemetery. I just sat there close by like a useless lump. Boy, was I a loser. Here was this person that I claimed was my best friend and would do anything I could to help, but when came down to it, I had nothing to offer. After the burial, I gave him a quick nod and a smile and got in my car and drove my worthless self home.

I remember feeling really bad about it, obsessing over why I couldn't find some great words of wisdom that could make things better like those guys did in the movies, but there I was—just plain old me. My first real test to show someone I cared about some sense of support, and I totally blew it.

Right about the time I was feeling the lowest, my sister Colleen came home. We have always been extremely close, and she could tell something was bothering me. After a little coaxing, I told her the story of my miserable failure and how I had let this person down so badly. She looked at me with the same familiar smile that I had grown to love over the years, and still do, and she simply said to me, "You know what, Timmy? Sometimes just being there is enough."

I have never forgotten those words, and really they have become a constant theme that I strive to live by.

"Be there, for everything, big and small. Just show up, be attentive, interested, and available." I show up for everything I can—all the family events, all the birthdays, all the games and recitals, even if only for a few minutes. I go because it lets the people that I care about the most know that they are important and that what's important to them is always going to be important to me. Sometimes I even have a few good words to say these days, but I know that is not really a necessity.

Have you been there for the people you care about? Have you shown up for the most important people in your life? There is always something else going on, always some reason not to do something. What are you really saying to those people you supposedly care so much about when you don't even bother to make an appearance for those important moments in their lives that they have asked you to be a part of? It really doesn't matter if it's not all that exciting or something that you are not really interested in, because guess what, it's not really about you. It really doesn't take all that much effort to just show up and pay attention.

Ask yourself:

- Where am I going to show up in a big way?
- Who have I not been there for recently?
- What am I going to do this week to remedy the situation?
- Where in my life can I just "be there"?

SCHEDULE IT!

I constantly get requests to speak or conduct sessions about time management and productivity, so I thought this would be an appropriate Quarter Turn topic, especially when it comes to strategy.

Are you aware of the "unprecedented numbers" of work hours being reported over the past few years, yet productivity hasn't increased? Some studies suggest we are actually less productive. By far the biggest killer of productivity is DISTRACTIONS! Yes, the little device that is buzzing in your pocket as you read this, the instant messenger you have beeping on your computer, a coworker that "pops in" and asks, "Do have a minute?" Those seemingly insignificant yet extremely common events, while helping you get your work done, are probably also causing some damaging side effects like stress, illness, sleep deprivation, anxiety, headaches, longer hours leading to less work/life balance. Sound familiar?

Here is an idea for creating the time you need to get your work done: SCHEDULE IT! That's right, if you have a project or task you are working on and it's important, then make an appointment with yourself on that little smartphone that you wield like a Samurai sword. You can even create an invite and send it to yourself for this important session.

Think about it logically for a minute. If you needed to go to the doctor, you wouldn't just "pop in" whenever you felt like it. You'd set up an appointment. I know many of you are probably thinking, "But what if it's an emergency?" I get it, and I realize that there are times you may have to skip making an appointment and head straight to the ER for serious unforeseen issues. The problem is that many treat their routine daily, weekly, and monthly tasks much like ER visits because they are not scheduling time to complete them. Consequently, you probably need an ambulance ride and major surgery to complete any new or special tasks that show up on your radar screen! You know it, and I know it, since I've coached many of you through your ER recoveries.

If you are anything like me, if it's not on your schedule or your calendar, then it probably doesn't exist in your world. My wife and I have started putting things on my calendar months in advance for family events and kids' sports. Events that we both know I'm going to want to attend. You could do the same for just about anything. Especially if you ever want to take a day off again someday! So if it's important, then schedule it, please, before you get another "meeting request" and before you dot another *i*, Bob Cratchit! If it's important enough, SCHEDULE IT! Please excuse me now, I need to go and check my e-mail.

I'm so happy that you've stayed with me up to this point and have been able to apply some Quarter Turns to your business and in your life. Now that we have developed some success strategies, it is time to move toward the most important phase, which is sustainability.

Section 5

Sustainability

I've often told people that I'm not interested in having a coaching client for life. The people that I work with live in an accelerated world and need real tools to get measurable results in a condensed period of time. That's the world that we live in, and I don't believe that's going to change any time in the near future.

You have started down the path of gaining awareness and clarity. You've identified some very real obstacles and have begun to develop a strategy to succeed in all areas of your life. Now it is time to create real, impactful, and sustainable change in your life. Reading this book could be an event that inspires you, or maybe that really "neat thing" you did that one time. Or it could be the beginning of a process that actually transforms you by allowing you to become this amazing person that has always lived within you. Which would be better for you?

Now that you have seen some results, how do you sustain it? How do you keep from reverting back to your old behaviors? We are human beings and creatures of habit. We develop new patterns and habits almost on a daily basis, so how do we sustain the Quarter Turns we have already made? Well, it starts by going back to the beginning and being aware.

Now that you are in tune with who you are and how you show up, it's much easier to recognize when you are not being consistent with the person you are becoming. What will be the signs that you are slipping? How will that feel? You know that feeling well because you have lived with it for many years.

Once you recognize that you are beginning to slip into old habits of allowing your obstacles to get in your way, get ready to apply the strategies that we have developed to keep moving in the direction you plan to go.

Look, we are all going to slip at times and do or say things we wish we hadn't. The growth is that we now recognize the behavior and where it's coming from, and from my perspective as a coach, that's a huge step in the right direction. This work isn't easy, and if it was then everyone would be successful.

Your job is to continue to apply those little Quarter Turns you've already learned and start looking for the new ones each and every day. I liken the work we are doing together to the game of golf. Golf is a game that isn't won or lost, it's simply played. Even if you've never played before, you've probably seen it or at least played putt-putt golf. Like golf, we usually know exactly what we are supposed to do, but there are days when we simply can't seem to figure it out. Then there are those days where every shot finds the fairway, every green is in reach, every hole looks much bigger, and that's why we keep playing.

How are you going to sustain the work you have started? How are you planning to keep playing this most important game at a very high level? These next Quarter Turns are designed to help answer those important questions.

Unplug from the Matrix

Every summer, my family and I like to take a vacation in northern Michigan. It's truly one of the most beautiful places on earth with its clear blue waters, sandy beaches, clean air, and quaint little tourist villages. It's an easy place to fall in love with.

There is one added benefit that I have only just come to acknowledge. Cell phone reception in this part of the world isn't all that great and impossible in some areas. I remember the first time I failed to get reception up there several years ago and how stressed I got about it, "Oh no! What if someone wants to get in contact with me, what if I'm needed, what am I going to do?"

It took me about a day or so before I finally accepted this as part of the experience, and I let go. Once I did, it felt REALLY GOOD! I was able to relax and enjoy time with my family, without a to-do list or an inbox. I was able to spend my days at a laid-back pace that is hard to come by in the modern world. I did it! I unplugged from the Matrix! I have done it every year since, and sometimes I don't even have to go to a remote place to do it.

Lately I have found myself being envious of my father and grandfather, because I can't remember my dad EVER taking a work call during dinner or at home in the evening, and certainly not on vacations. I don't remember him glued to a cell phone or a computer when he wasn't in his office. I am so jealous of that era, because I know those days are probably never coming back.

So my question for you is: Where can you go today to unplug for one hour? Try these options: a massage, a coffee shop, a park bench, working out, a room with no television . . .

Ask yourself:

- How can I unplug from the Matrix?
- Where is the best place for me to do so?
- If I feel it's impossible, what steps am I going to take in my business and in my life to ensure that I get this time to unplug?

Once you find that time, I can almost guarantee it will be the time that you value the most.

Delegating versus Micromanaging

Are you truly delegating or just telling people what to do and then micromanaging the situation? While many leaders believe they are delegating, most struggle with handing off basic tasks to their teams. In my coaching practice, I have worked with so many who made the jump into a leadership position, and I can tell you unequivocally that most of them struggle to let go of the tasks they were once responsible for every day to the person they are now charged with leading.

What is the leader actually saying to the person by not giving up this task or responsibility to the team member? "You are not good enough! I don't trust you! You can't possibly handle this responsibility!" Is that really the impact you want to have on your teams?

These unspoken messages in turn cause the team to do less, be unproductive, and become resentful of their leader. As this occurs, the leader takes on more and more responsibility, focusing less on the goals and vision of the department and devoting more time to doing the actual tasks. As this happens, the work suffers, the department becomes less productive, and the leader begins to resent the team members for not stepping up and doing their part. Sound familiar, everyone? By the way, this also leads to tension, stress, work/life imbalance, unsustainable output, and corporate burnout!

If you have ever had the pleasure of actually hiring someone for a position or offering him/her a promotion, I can tell you it's a pretty amazing experience. Even if you haven't hired someone, you yourself have been offered a position, and it feels pretty good, doesn't it? In that moment, I can almost guarantee you that no one is thinking, "Boy, I can't wait to come and work here so that I can sit around and do nothing!" That is a learned behavior. If you have someone like that on your team, then start by asking yourself, "What have I done to create this situation?"

You might be worried that this person will make a mistake or screw something up, and it's natural to want to help because that's what you have always done.

Think back to when you had the job that you now manage, when you had a problem or challenge, did you go running to your boss and ask him/her to do it for you? No! You figured it out, right? Did you ever make a mistake? Yes! Did you learn from it? Yes! My first coach used to say, "You never learn anything in this life until you have had your head handed to you a few times!" Isn't that true? But we are so worried about employees making mistakes that we go overboard and just do it for them. That's not leading, not sustainable, and certainly not going to get you the impact you are intending or build a high-performing, productive team.

Ask yourself:

- How am I delegating tasks to my team?
- Am I allowing those I delegate to make mistakes?
- How am I using those mistakes to coach for performance-based solutions?
- Am I coaching or just telling them what to do?
- Do I ask questions and empower my team members, or am I too busy fixing and solving problems with my brilliant intellect?
- What or whom am I willing to commit to this week to start really delegating and stopping the insanity?

Developing Your Bench Strength

Having two sons that are very active in sports can be a full-time job, especially for my wife. I always do my best to arrange my travel schedule around their game calendars. It never ceases to amaze me all of the Quarter Turns that come to me as a result of their participation with their teams. Not to mention how much fun I have watching them play.

As I've mentioned, my oldest son, Dylan, loves baseball and plays on a travel team that has been together for the past five years. This past year was a bit challenging as some of the older boys were eligible to play JV baseball for their respective high schools, which, by the way, is the goal of most travel organizations—to prepare the kids to play high school ball.

Unfortunately, they are not allowed to play on their travel teams during the high school season due to state rules, so this left Dylan's team a bit shorthanded the first month of the season. As a result, many of the kids were asked to play positions that they had never experienced before, and my son volunteered to play catcher.

It didn't seem to bother him much that he's the smallest kid on the field at all times (and due to the genetics of his parents, probably always will be) or that he's one of the team's best middle infielders.

Having never played catcher before, it took some getting used to, and initially Dylan looked a bit like a fish out of water. Much to my surprise, he really embraced his temporary new role on the team and has developed into a decent catcher.

After one of the games, we had a long drive home, and Dylan and I were able to have a conversation about his experience as a catcher. He talked about how at first he was really nervous but that playing a different position had given him an entirely new perspective on how the plays unfold and how important positioning is with throws coming in from the outfield.

He talked about how physically demanding being the catcher was and how he has a new appreciation for his teammates that play this position. He liked the proximity to players on the other team and how each player had a unique approach to hitting. He was able to gain new perspective of how the strike zone expands and contracts during the course of the game.

The most important lesson was being able to chat with the umpires constantly and realizing that these were just regular guys that loved the game and were doing the best they could to help younger kids learn and grow. He realized that they weren't just guys dressed in blue, put on this earth to screw up his life by blowing close calls that determined the outcomes of games.

After this conversation I began thinking about many of the companies that I work with and just how valuable it is to get a cross section of people from different departments into the same room to discuss challenges and offer their perspectives on them.

How often do we segregate areas of our organizations, whether intentionally or unintentionally, and what outcomes do we get from that? How are we depriving our teams of the perspectives of others? Where are we allowing our teams to get comfortable only thinking about their own roles?

How much would it help grow our organizations if we were to allow groups to cross-pollinate and experience the company from another position—even if just for a day? Not so they can actually learn how to do someone else's job, but so they appreciate the unique challenges that these other jobs hold.

Would our team members benefit from understanding that others in the organization are not just lumps of matter with an "@.com" attached to their name? That these people are not put here on this earth to identify ways to make our lives more difficult or hamper our productivity? They are real people with real lives, and they do their jobs every day with the hope of contributing value to the organization that they serve. That's bench strength, and that is what creates sustainability.

Ask yourself:

- What am I doing to develop the bench strength in my organization?
- How am I allowing my teams to gain an appreciation of other departments and divisions?
- Where are the individual silos in my organization and how am I addressing them?
- In what area of my life or business do I personally need to gain a new perspective?

Chutes and Ladders

Are you on track with the goals you've set for yourself? If you are not on track, that's okay. Think of this as a guide marker to help push you back in the direction you want to go. Remember, the road to your goals is rarely a perfectly straight line. You will drift and fall off track. Just make sure you have guide markers and compass points to help keep you moving the direction you want to go.

In one of my Mastermind Groups, we were discussing that very topic as one of our participants was feeling a bit down and frustrated that she had slipped so far off the path she had set for herself—especially after making so much progress and coming so far.

I started to use the analogy of an airplane. Once the aircraft gets off the ground, the autopilot usually takes over, and every hour the computer makes thousands of tiny course corrections based on air pressure, outside temperature, wind speed, weight, air traffic, and a host of other variables. Even though the destination is clearly plugged in, the aircraft will drift off course.

We are the same way. Even with our clearly stated goals and outcomes, we will drift off course, because hey, that's life, and we are human. The goal here is not to drift so far off track that we crash and burn spectacularly, which many of us have done, including me. That's why it's so important to have a support group, a coach or mentor, and real-world strategies to keep yourself energized and focused when you fall down and slam into the pavement.

At that moment, one insightful Mastermind participant stated, "It's just like a game of Chutes and Ladders!"

What a great example of our daily experience. You remember that board game you played in elementary school? It was one of my favorites. It's the game where you keep moving up the ramp, back and forth, like Donkey Kong. Every so often you get to take a shortcut up the ladder a level or two, and you're feeling really good about your progress. Then all of a sudden you land on the chute or the slide that takes you down a level or two, sometimes all the way back to the start.

It's frustrating, and you wonder to yourself, "Why does this keep happening? I'm smart, and I thought I already learned this lesson." Eventually, you get back on the path and keep moving in the direction you originally planned. It's just a lot easier when you know EXACTLY where you are going, and you have a team of supporters and strategies to rely on to get you up off the floor and going back in the right direction.

The road to success is never a straight line; it's more like a game of Chutes and Ladders!

Ask yourself:

- Where in my life have I drifted off course from my destination?
- How have I responded to one of my recent setbacks?
- What support system do I have in place for sustainability and to help get me back on track?
- What can I do this week to start climbing back up the ladder?

Take a Snow Day

I travel extensively, and living in Michigan can make the winter months a bit hectic due to weather conditions. Flights can be delayed or cancelled. The rental car isn't designed for snow, and hotels are overbooked. As I'm stressing out, I usually start wondering why I choose to live in Michigan. Then my kids remind me—snow days!

Any of you that grew up in a cold-weather state know just how exciting a snow day can be. My kids would start bouncing off the walls, deciding how late they were going to stay up and what the plans were for the next day. I get excited myself just watching them.

Sometimes, when my planned schedule gets shot due to unexpected weather or events, I take the day off as well to enjoy a snow day with them. I realize how disconnected we can all become from the simple things that used to give us so much joy.

In the hustle of our jobs, our careers, and our daily experiences, we sometimes tend to forget it's the little things that really count, that we remember, and that make all the difference.

So every once in a while, take a snow day, a rain day, or even a heat day, and make sure to do it with those that you care about the most!

Traditions

Traditions are so valuable. I don't know where they all came from or how they started, but once they start, they sure are exciting. Having traditions is something to look forward to, and they can sustain us when we are having those difficult days.

My dad and I have gone to high school basketball tournaments in the state of Ohio since I was in about sixth or seventh grade. Every year we go for a few days. We watch basketball. We make our bets. We talk ball. We get a "reading" (my dad's take on what is happening).

The basketball to me is really secondary because the time that we spend together is what's so valuable. As I've gotten older, it's gotten harder to make that commitment to get down there. It seems like every year when it comes around, I say I'm not going to go, but I always go, and I'm always thankful that I did.

I come from a large family where traditions make up the fabric of life. Every year, on the day after Thanksgiving, my entire extended family has a football game. Everyone participates in it, and we've gotten to the point where all of our kids participate too. Now it's not only the Thanksgiving holiday, but it's also the family football game, and it's become something that the kids look forward to. My hope is that someday our kids' children will want to play that game as well.

My wife and I have started many traditions with our family. One of my favorites, which started right after we were married, is putting up our Christmas tree while eating our favorite types of seafood and listening to the Harry Connick Jr. Christmas CD all night. Over the years the seafood has gotten much fancier and our wine no longer comes from a box, but for the most part this tradition stays the same and is made even better with our kids now part of it.

These traditions are a very real part of our lives and really the glue that binds us together. They're important and make us who we are. When I really stop to think about it, we are the sum of our traditions. That's how we sustain ourselves. We are made up of our habits and things that we've done or look forward to. What you do on Christmas Eve or that special holiday and the annual rituals and events you have with your family (like sitting down to dinner and celebrating life) is tradition and habit. These habits become something that is important.

So don't miss those traditions. Make an effort to get there even when it's inconvenient.

My definition of a tradition is something that you do even when maybe you don't feel like it; even sometimes when it's inconvenient, you make the effort and you do it. And when you're done, you're always thankful for it.

Ask yourself:

- What are my favorite traditions?
- With whom do I share my best traditions?
- What new traditions would I like to create?

Great Players Make Lots of Good Plays

I was listening to a basketball coach answer questions about his team on a sports talk radio program. The team was underachieving. The conversation was focused around the performance of the team's star player and why he wasn't scoring the way he had in previous years. The coach responded:

"You know great players make lots of good plays, and sometimes those good plays do not show up in points or rebounds or assists."

That statement really resonated with me after I replayed it back in my head a few times. First of all, I appreciated how quick he was to defend his young star and how he was quick to give credit to him for all the little things he did besides score. This statement also served another purpose, as it sent a strong message to the rest of his team as well.

In our society, we are so conditioned to only celebrate the superstar that rarely do we take the time to appreciate those on our teams that maybe aren't as flashy or polished. Those individuals who are not in the spotlight gaining all the credit and accolades still need reinforcement that they contribute to the overall success of the team. That's how you sustain a high performing team.

We can get so concerned about top performers that it's easy to forget about all the role players and bench players that show up and make those "really good plays" every single day. Unfortunately, our stat sheets in sports, business, and life only show the obvious successes, but as we have learned, it's the little wins or Quarter Turns that often go unnoticed by others that can be the most satisfying.

Challenge yourself to:

- Recognize the good plays made by yourself and others around you.
- Celebrate the little wins in private or in public.
- Take the time to notice your stars doing the little things that help the team win.
- Thank a role player in your business or your life for helping sustain the success of the team!

Give Credit where Credit Is Due

Successful people are very quick to give others credit without discounting what they themselves bring to the table. I'm talking about people who can put their egos aside for the moment and give others credit for work they've done and allow others to be recognized and share the spotlight along with them.

The reverse is those people who are quick to give credit to everyone else yet can never take credit for anything they have done themselves. These people give, give, give, give, but act as though they're never doing anything or bringing anything to the table.

Do you see the big difference?

What I'm talking about are those people who genuinely give credit to others when they've done something, allow others to share that recognition, be recognized, and feel good in that moment.

I've learned that the people who give more credit in this manner tend to get more credit. Isn't that interesting? Those who give others genuine, heartfelt credit tend to get more credit themselves for the teams they've built and for the people they've developed, and they tend to be very successful.

It's a simple concept yet often in practice it falls short. If you overdo it, it can feel fake or disingenuous. It can also alienate others around you if they don't feel they are getting the credit they deserve.

If you are focused and intentional, then you really can give credit to others without overdoing it, as well as earn yourself some credit without shortchanging either of you in the process.

Allowing others to bask in the glory of success and realizing that their credit does not come at the expense of yours is harder than it sounds. But when you can truly give credit without discounting yourself, I think you'll be surprised at how much credit actually comes back to you.

Ask yourself:

- Do I give an honest, heartfelt thank you to everyone who does something that helps me?
- Do I tell others about the good performance of one of my team members, coworkers, or employees?
- Do I write e-mails or notes for management that explain the positive contributions of others?

Start to give credit and watch your own account grow!

Celebrate Success

It never ceases to amaze me how many of us choose to dismiss the big goals or even the little goals that we accomplish. We fire through them, get them finished, check off the box, and move on to the next one. We never take a minute to just say, "Wow. What a great job." Where in your life are you not celebrating success?

I'm not even talking about the big items, the home runs in life, because they are few and far between. By the way, if you're constantly waiting for home runs in your life or your business to do that little celebration, to do your touchdown dance, then you're totally missing out, because most of the best achievements in life, the best opportunities for celebration, are the little things.

John Lennon once wrote, "Life is what happens while you're busy making other plans."

The little milestones that you accomplish every day are where life is lived most of the time. Yet, it seems we just meander through them or blow them off every day like they're meaningless. I call it "check the box mentality."

Wouldn't it be great if we walked into the office and there was a cheering section? Like an athlete or musician walking into an arena with everyone screaming, "Yeah! There he/she is!" I sometimes wish that when I got home and walked through the door that my wife and kids would shout, "Yeah! There's Dad!" Unfortunately, at least for most of us, that doesn't usually happen. So if you're missing out on that opportunity to say to yourself, "Hey, you know what? Nice job," then you're missing out on some big opportunities to experience that satisfying sense of fulfillment that comes with accomplishment.

I come across so many talented individuals that appear hollowed out and have an absolute inability to celebrate anything they accomplish.

Let me ask you a question: If you don't celebrate success, then who will? When in your life do you ever get to cross the goal line, spike the ball, and do your touchdown dance? When do you get to give yourself that well-deserved pat on the back? Do it this week. It is fun, it is worthwhile, and it does mean something.

I'm not saying that after every little thing you do that you have to go crazy, but it's important to recognize these little wins and not just check the box and move on to the next one because that's what we've become accustomed to doing. "Well, I got that done, now on to the next one." Your life is a lot more than just a list of items to check off.

The idea of appreciating the little things is very powerful to sustain the enthusiasm and endurance needed to accomplish the big things. In addition to giving you a moment to feel good, it gives you a chance to decide what to do next. That extra moment you take to decide what to do next gives you a chance to reassess your priorities and reconsider your goals, big and small. It also allows you to assess your performance and take note of methods to improve.

The risk of doing a self-assessment is the potential for unnecessarily harsh criticism. Wanting to get better should not be used as an excuse to beat yourself up and say, "Oh God, I can't believe I didn't do this. I'm so stupid. I can't believe it took me so long."

Quiet that internal "ass-kicking mechanism" and instead use the opportunity to say, "Okay, here's a chance to look back at how I did that. How can I improve the process? How could I have done this a little differently? I would have enlisted this person's help. I would have gotten that information sooner."

Mentally take that note, or even write it down so that the next time you will do it. But don't get bogged down with, "Oh man, I can't believe I did this or that."

Make sure the conversation you are having with yourself is honest and constructive. If you find yourself becoming demoralized, you are not helping yourself. So check that conversation, celebrate those successes, and when you get a chance, do your touchdown dance.

Ask yourself:

- Where in my life am I failing to celebrate success?
- How is that impacting my life, my business, or my relationships?
- Where have I become a check-the-box type of person?
- When am I going to get to do my crazy little touchdown dance?

Welcoming Your New Addition

So we welcomed a new addition to our family recently. No, it's not what you think. We are the proud parents of a three-month-old, four-pound baby fluff ball Pomeranian puppy named Desmond. After years of begging from my two boys and my wife, I finally relented, and I have to say he is really cute. I haven't had a puppy in the house since I was in grade school, and over the past few weeks I'm beginning to realize one thing . . . new puppies are a hell of a lot of WORK!

Before we brought him home, we had a really great plan on how to potty train him, where he would sleep, how we would behave, and all sorts of grand ideas about bringing him into the family. Well, as I'm sure you can guess, Desmond seems to have a mind of his own, and his plan is completely different from ours.

Just when we think he has something figured out the way we want him to, he goes off and tears into a new pair of shoes. One week he is going outside to do his business, the next week he has found a corner in the living room that seems to suit his needs much better. The minute we take our eyes off him, he's off doing something he shouldn't be doing. I have to tell you, I'm exhausted!

While my guess is you're entertained with our new puppy exploits, you're probably wondering how any of this is relevant to you and your business.

Well, I'm sure you're aware the economy is beginning to pick up some momentum. In fact, over the past few years, many of the organizations I work with have slowly begun to hire new team members and fill badly needed positions to meet the growing demands of the business. Many of you are about to add new people to your teams, and I'm sure you're as excited about that as my family was about our new addition. Once that excitement wanes, however, you'll be reminded, as I have been, that adding a new employee is a tremendous responsibility and a ton of work.

Think about all the ways your new team member will need to get acclimated to their new role, not to mention the particular nuances of your business and your team. How will they get along with the rest of the team? How will they know what to do? It's easy to assume that your new hire will "just know" what to do and where to go because they don't stop and ask for help. Mistakes are made by concluding, "They must know, because they didn't ask." Consider instead whether you've made it clear to them that it's OK to ask, that you expect them to ask rather than wonder, assume, or guess.

Do you remember what it's like to be the new person? How willing were you to step up and say, "I don't understand." Also, just because they get something right doesn't mean you don't have to validate and reinforce their understanding to make sure it sticks. You know from experience that the minute you take your eye off of them, they may make a mess all over your workplace, or worse, get lost or run away out of frustration.

Yes, my friends, if you're getting ready to make some additions to your teams in the coming months, remember it's a lot like getting that new puppy. Even if you have a well thought out plan, remember that people are unique, and their plan may be a bit different from your plan. The good news is that if you put in the effort early on, stay after them to create the right habits from day one (without micromanaging), and treat them with dignity and respect, then they will pay you back ten times the amount with a lifetime of loyalty, productivity, and happiness!

Ask yourself:

- How am I preparing for my new addition to the workplace?
- What training have I set up to help them succeed?
- How much of my own time have I set aside to invest in this new team member?
- What are my plans to let them know that it's OK to ask for help; that it's good to ask for help?

Leadership Lessons from Subway Subs

For my oldest son's fourteenth birthday, he invited a few friends to go bowling. They wanted to get Subway for dinner and head home to watch some horror movies. A perfect night for a young teenager, right? My wife is a personal trainer, so Subway is the only option available in our family as far as fast food goes, which is fine by me as I like it myself. I enjoy watching people make their strange sandwich orders, and I am always amazed at the interesting combinations of veggies and toppings that are so unique to each individual.

If you have a teenage boy, then you probably know that most of them aren't too adventuresome when it comes to sandwiches. Ham and cheese or turkey and cheese with maybe some lettuce or mayo seems to be the most common choice when it comes to these boys.

You can imagine my surprise when one of my son's friends, Trevor, ordered up a pepperoni sandwich, with cheese, peppers, lettuce, and mustard. My stomach started aching just thinking about it. I even asked him if he was sure that's what he wanted, and he said, "Oh yes, that's what I always have." As they were munching them down, I watched him devour his sandwich with a lot of pride and pleasure. Whatever I thought about his decision was irrelevant, because it sure seemed to work for him.

Later on that evening I began thinking about the thousands of people in leadership positions that I've had the privilege to work with and coach and thought to myself, "Leadership is a lot like going to Subway." Think about it: we are all given so many amazing tools that we can work with to lead and manage our businesses and ourselves. Each and every one of those tools has value and, when combined with others, can create energy and momentum to grow and sustain our teams and our businesses.

Much like the toppings at Subway, there is no single combination that is universally accepted as "the way" to do it, and in fact what works for some may or may not work for others—and that's OK. The beauty is we get to keep adding and testing out combinations until we hit on the right formula that has the impact we desire. What's most important is that the combination you choose works for you, and as long as you get the outcomes you are looking for, then why change it?

The second part of this is how we react or respond when others choose to lead differently than we do. If they choose to top off their leadership with lettuce, mayo, peppers, and their own secret sauce, then we have to be OK with that as well. As human beings, it's our nature to judge and superimpose our own solutions and how we would do things onto those around us, but as leaders it's incumbent upon us to allow others to learn, lead, and grow in the ways best suited to their own uniqueness.

By the way, as far as I'm concerned, the only way to have Subway is with turkey, Swiss, lettuce, tomatoes, pickles, banana peppers, mustard, and just a bit of that sweet onion sauce all on untoasted honey oat bread!

Ask yourself:

- What is my special combination of leadership skills that gets me the outcomes I'm looking for?
- What is my secret sauce for sustainability?

- Who am I imposing my own ingredients on when the ones they are using seem to work just fine for them?
- Where else in my life am I allowing my way to be the only way? How's that working for me?

Wake-Up Call

My first coach used to always tell me that "your life is not a dress rehearsal," and I've added to that the phrase "we won't get a do-over!" What are we waiting for?

Too many in this world are living life half asleep, uncommitted to their own success, unwilling to let go of outdated belief systems, and accepting mediocrity. I heard it said before: "There is a lot of competition for mediocrity, that space is full, but there is very little competition for exceptional!" I believe in living life by design and on purpose. What about you?

Over the course of reading this book, you have received a wake-up call and a new set of eyes through which to view your life and the world around you. What do you plan to do now that you are wide awake and focused? Now is the time for you to take charge of your life and your business in a big way. Keep the momentum going, and make those small Quarter Turns every day and every week. Stop waiting for something to happen and start making something happen! The choice is 100 percent yours, so make a good one!

Ask yourself:

- What was my wake-up call?
- What Quarter Turn has had an impact on my life or my business?

Who Are You Now?

I'm so honored that you have chosen to come along on this ride with me. I have a few questions for you, the same questions that I ask of everyone that has gotten this far.

What are you going to take away from this journey?

Through this process, my belief is that an evolution has occurred in your thinking and your approach to many aspects of your life. Who are you now? Describe yourself. What Quarter Turns have you made? How have you applied them, and what has been the impact—at home, at work, and in your relationships? Are you moving closer to the person you want to be? What do your goals and big rocks look like now? What is your personal brand?

What will you do now that is different from before? What actions will you take to honor the person you have become? Take a moment to describe the actions that you took that are an extension of the person you want to be.

My hope is that you have found some value and been able to relate to and apply some of my personal Quarter Turns in your life. My real wish is that you will start to notice the Quarter Turns that are happening in your own life every day. The great gift of Quarter Turns is that they are all around us and show up every day in so many different ways. We only need to tune in and pay attention to the lessons they are teaching us. It's these lessons that create the opportunity to make the tiny shifts, minor adjustments, course corrections, and Quarter Turns, enabling us to achieve our highest potential.

Thank you and here's to your continued success, one Quarter Turn at a time.

A Gift for You

Want to continue your journey? Take my Free 10-Day Coaching Challenge and find out how coaching can help you achieve your goals at the highest levels: MyQuarterTurns.com/free-virtual-coaching. For new Quarter Turns, please visit my website at MyQuarterTurns.com

Here's to your continued success, one Quarter Turn at a time.

Looking forward to our next conversation.

Tim Furlong

One Small Request

My mission is to impact the lives of one million people and this book is a big part of helping achieve that goal. I am so honored and humbled that you have chosen to invest in yourself by purchasing this book or following the Quarter Turn articles at MyQuarterTurns.com. Would you please do me one favor and post a review of the book on Amazon? That will help me move closer to my goal of going platinum and impacting a bigger audience. I am truly grateful and blessed for your continued support!

Thank you!

Here's to your continued success, one Quarter Turn at a time.

Acknowledgements

Naming all of the people that made this book a reality is impossible because many of them I observed in my coaching, training, travels, family events, or simply running errands. However, there are a few individuals that deserve acknowledgement because they really helped write this book. AnnMarie, Dylan, and Jake—my three favorite people on the planet and the reason I will always strive to be a better person, husband, father, and friend. Karen, Maureen, Kevin, Mark, and Colleen—my safety net, back-stop, and support system that always gave me the courage to put myself out there and go for it. "Awesome Ann"—for believing in my talent and ability, fostering the environment, and creating so many opportunities for success. Alan—the yin to my mother's yang and the rock of our family. Fuzz and Donna—who didn't come-a-learning, but came-a-knowing. John—for showing me a life after the music stopped playing. Bob—who opened the door to an entire new world and introduced me to a different kind of coach. Fred—for teaching me how to tap into my energy and focus on what is important. Greta, Mike, Stephen, and Sam—for keeping us all sane and getting our ducks in a row.

Eric, Luke, Julia, and Jamie; Andy, Kelly, and John; Ryan, Kim, Brin, and Sarah; Chris and Vanessa; Melinda; Lisa and Mike; Steve and Becky; Amy and Matt; Tom and Jeri; Beth and David— for sharing this amazing journey and being a part of my life.

Andy—for believing in this project, believing in me, and helping push this into the end-zone, I can't thank you enough. Rob—for keeping me honest and challenging me in ways you will never really know.

And finally to all of those out there who have entrusted me to coach, train, speak, and mentor you and your organizations, I thank you from the bottom of my heart. Most of the stories and thoughts can be traced back to the conversations and discussions I've been privileged to be a part of with all of you!

About the Author

Tim Furlong

"Train, Retain, and Sustain High Performing Teams and Individuals"

A nationally recognized speaker, facilitator, and executive coach, Tim Furlong and his unique brand of "edutainment" have impacted nearly every type of organization for nearly two decades. The Hard Rock Hotels and Casinos, M&Ms Mars, Whole Foods, Michael Kors, the National Parks Service, New York Life, MTV, VH1, the University of Michigan Athletic Department, and the NHL's Nashville Predators are just a few of the broad range of organizations that have chosen to utilize Tim and his dynamic, insightful presentations. Tim is also the creator and founder of the Quarter Turns coaching program, which enables leaders in any industry to identify small shifts in approach and behavior that yield highly impactful, sustainable results. From CEOs of Fortune 500 companies to platinum-selling recording artists, Tim's coaching and training programs empower thousands of individuals and organizations to achieve at the highest levels.

MyQuarterTurns.com
Coach.tim@me.com
734-216-7306

Made in the USA
Columbia, SC
03 April 2019